JULIE DAVIS

AUTHOR OF
30 DAYS TO A BEAUTIFUL BOTTOM

365 DIET TIPS

PROVEN ADVICE FROM DIETERS COAST TO COAST: A HINT A DAY TO MELT THOSE POUNDS— AND KEEP THEM AWAY!

BALLANTINE BOOKS • NEW YORK

Copyright © 1985 by Julie Davis

All rights reserved under International and Pan-American Copyright Conventions. Published in the United States by Ballantine Books, a division of Random House, Inc., New York, and simultaneously in Canada by Random House of Canada Limited, Toronto.

Library of Congress Catalog Card Number: 84-90933

ISBN 0-345-31848-X

Manufactured in the United States of America

First Edition: January 1985

Tip #28: If you have a hard time staying on a diet for even one week, diet by the day.

Tip #229: Give yourself $5 for every week you stick with your diet.

Tip #231: To renew your incentive, do your swimsuit shopping in January and February.

Tip #259: Find a private retreat in your home, one you can escape to when family members go on a binge by the TV.

Tip #307: The next time you need a morale boost, treat yourself to a manicure or pedicure.

Tip #345: Incorporate two of your top ten "love" foods into your weekly maintenance menus.

Also by Julie Davis
Published by Ballantine Books:

HOW TO GET MARRIED
  (with Dr. Herman Weiss)

TABLE OF CONTENTS

v

ACKNOWLEDGMENTS

This book represents the combined efforts of a fantastic group of people who shared their proven "secrets" of weight loss—techniques, strategies, even mind games they played with themselves, all in the name of dieting. They deserve not only thanks but congratulations for going where few men and women dare to tread: on a new, *lifelong* eating course. The assistance of Sally Mitlitzky, my diet buddy, was unparalleled; she pushed me to lose weight and to write this book, offering hours of time in developing tips and going over each and every one. Maxine and Michael Breslauer, a dieting couple who together lost more than 130 pounds, explained how their buddy system worked so successfully, and gave their time and encouragement as well. Equal praise goes to the rest of our ad hoc diet panel—successful "losers" all: Amy Davenport and Greg Papa, Phyllis Goldstein, Roberta Yafie, Rochelle Larkin, Ronald Davis, Nancy and Billy Schnabel, Paul Gellman, Lynne Klinghoffer, Annemarie Wurche, and Renata Renner. And a special thank you to Mike Wolf, a terrific friend who gave his professional nod to the message each one of us had: exercise. May we all see brownies in our dreams, but not on our bottoms!

AN INTRODUCTION

365 DIET TIPS is not another diet book—in fact, it doesn't contain a diet at all. *365 Diet Tips* is an encyclopedia of diet advice designed to be your primary weapon in the battle of weight loss. It is a pocket companion to supplement whatever diet you're on and make it more effective. *365 Diet Tips* works at keeping you on track as you diet week in and week out—you won't feel abandoned after 7 to 14 days as you do with most diet plans. *365 Diet Tips* goes the distance with you! It is a calendar of tips: one for every day of your diet and beyond, showing you how to keep off your lost pounds (a goal diet books fall far short of).

365 DIET TIPS provides advice from the real experts— not dieticians or diet doctors but former fatties, myself included! As the author of numerous books on beauty, health, and fitness, I knew that exercise and sound calorie counting added up to weight loss. But as a dieter with over 30 pounds to lose, I found that there had to be more to dieting than that to be successful. Staying on a diet requires sustained effort—constant reinforcement through motivation-boosting techniques. I had to devise my own strategies, because no diet book provided enough hints to maintain a strong resolve after the first week or two. And I found that most other successful dieters have done the same—improvised their own incentives, even tricks, in order to reach their weight loss goal. Seventeen of us—representing a collective loss of more than 450 pounds!—banded to form a diet panel to create this book. We charted what we did and why it worked, from tools for motivation to creating recipes, from researching diet aids to taste testing new food products. Our tips aren't textbook jargon—each one is a tried-and-true step to achieving permanent weight loss. We know because we've each been there!

365 DIET TIPS is for every dieter who wants to lose weight faster and as painlessly as possible. Its approach is realistic: I know from experience that you're going to want a piece of chocolate cake during your diet. *365 Diet Tips* tells you how to have it, how to resist having more, even how to get back on course should you have too much and go off your diet!—real-life advice the so-called "authorities" ignore.

365 DIET TIPS puts you in control; you decide how best to use its information:

- Make it your weight loss "bible"—it covers every aspect of dieting, from how to develop willpower to getting over a plateau to living with a spouse who loves cookies by the pound.
- Reach for it instead of a jelly donut whenever the craving strikes.
- Turn to a specific chapter as needed *or* read it straight through, cover to cover, *or* select one tip each day to integrate into your diet life-style— one *manageable* tip: *365 Diet Tips* doesn't ask you to turn your life upside down as many diet plans do!

I've based *365 DIET TIPS* on a 5-point weight loss objective:

1. **Decrease calories.** Fads or gimmicks won't do it; cutting back on portions and keeping careful track of calories is what sheds those unwanted pounds.

2. **Increase exercise.** Overweight is the result of too much intake, too little expenditure; getting physical balances the scales in your favor.

3. **Approach food in a new and healthful way.** Revise the way you deal with food, from buying right to cooking light, and keep a watchful eye toward nutrition to keep from getting that run-down feeling that could tempt you off your diet.

4. **Make a life-style change with behavior modification.** Replace eating with activity to change the habits that created the overweight and to break the psychological attachment you have toward food.

5. **Adopt a positive mental diet.** Become dedicated and motivated by using dieter's logic to stay with your system—forget the old rules and learn how to talk, cajole, even trick yourself into being "good."

Start to apply these principles and the following 365 diet tips right away. Use the guidelines and strategies to set up your own weight loss system or use only those tips that work with the diet you're now following. Each tip brings you closer to the results you want.... Together they work to make the diet you're on your last!

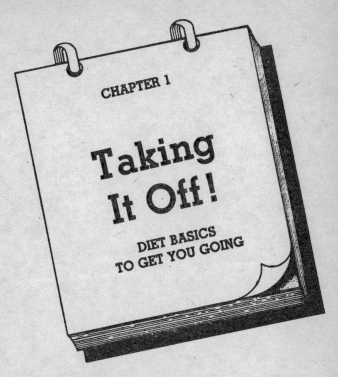

CHAPTER 1

Taking It Off!

DIET BASICS TO GET YOU GOING

The most effective diets are those based on principles of good nutrition to help you maintain good health as you lose. These tips show you how to cut back and eat right without sacrificing nutrients. Use them to perfect the diet you're on or to structure your own weight loss plan.

From now on, make "eat-to-live" your new approach to food.

TIP #1

This is a very different way of thinking from the live-to-eat habits of most overweight people. Quite different and quite necessary to change the underlying causes of your overweight and permanently correct the problem. So renounce your membership in the Clean Plate Club and teach yourself to eat only the minimum amounts required to sustain life—an average of 1200 calories a day for women, 1500 calories for men on a weight reduction program.

Keep a mental picture of a thin you in the front of your mind.

TIP #2

Of course it is dieting, or limiting your food intake, that helps bring about weight loss, but before you go through the physical motions of a diet, you need to improve your mental outlook by thinking thin and by imagining yourself at your goal, with a thin body. Once you can picture your results, you are in the right frame of mind to make them a reality. One successful dieter advises tuning into this mental image just before falling asleep—she wakes every morning with renewed determination, having "slept on" the positive reasons for dieting.

 Resist trying supposedly overnight solutions to overweight.

TIP #3

Stop looking for miracle gimmicks that promise unbelievable results. Instead realize that dieting is difficult and takes time. Once you accept this most hard-to-swallow fact, you will be on your way to becoming thin, a slow but steady route that will bring results. On the other hand, following weight loss fads is mere backtracking.

Invest in an accurate and comprehensive calorie book.

TIP #4

To get the most variety in your diet, you need to be able to calculate the caloric value of every food—charts that come in most diet books are too sketchy to be of real value. A good volume will give explicit information, not just an average calorie count for a potato, for instance, but per ounce raw and cooked in a variety of ways. The more precisely you can calculate your intake, the faster you can lose weight. Conversely, guesswork usually adds up to too many calories consumed each day, and that will naturally slow your progress. An excellent choice is Barbara Kraus' *Calories and Carbohydrates* (Grosset & Dunlap, Inc., 1971).

Vary your caloric intake within a 1000 to 1400 calorie-a-day range for women, 1300 to 1800 for men.

TIP #5

This keeps your metabolism (the rate at which your body uses calories) from getting stuck at a low set point and gives you leverage in meal planning, making your diet less monotonous.

To get yourself off to a flying start when a long-term diet is your plan, look for professional assistance for the first 2 weeks.

Once you acknowledge that you'll need to change your eating habits over a lengthy period of time, the good feelings of changing for the better can often be overshadowed by the depressing thought of a long sacrifice. To give your morale a shot in the arm, adopt a quick weight loss program for 14 days. Three options for this are: a trip to a weight loss community, such as Structure House in Durham, North Carolina (919-688-7379); a supervised fast conducted by your doctor; Weight Watchers' new Quick Start program. Rapid weight loss isn't the way to conduct your entire diet, but it can, at the very start, give you the impetus to go the full distance by giving you almost immediate results.

 When choosing a diet plan, look for one that tells you how to practice weight control once you've reached your desired size.

Without the guidelines for keeping weight off, a diet is incomplete.

 Satisfy your snacking urges with a mini-meal diet.

If you are a confirmed nibbler, the standard 3-meal-a-day regimen won't work for you. For success, adapt the diet of your choice to your eating pattern by dividing each meal in half and spreading these 6 "mini-meals" over the course of your day. With only 2 or 3 hours between meals instead of the usual 4 to 8, you will find it easier to adjust to a reduced calorie plan.

TIP #9

Put a check on your selective memory by keeping a diet journal.

On a small spiral notepad, write out each day's menu, complete with your specific diet's portion sizes and calorie count. This system lets you know exactly what you can eat and, as you check off each meal as consumed, lets you know where you stand at every hour of the day with a quick glance. Here is a sample listing:

Monday, 24th:

8 A.M.	4 oz orange juice	55
	1 cup dry cereal with 4 oz fat-free milk	150
noon	4 oz sliced cold chicken on 2 slices of bread	350
	4 oz mushrooms marinated in diet dressing	35
4 P.M.	4 oz 99% fat-free cottage cheese	90
	4 oz strawberries	40
8 P.M.	6 oz broiled flounder	135
	1 baked potato with fresh chives and	140
	¼ tbsp of butter	25
10 P.M.	1 7-oz banana	<u>120</u>
		1140

Take an hour each Saturday afternoon to draw up a 7-day menu plan for the upcoming week.

Daily meal planning is a hassle and makes it hard to limit supermarket trips. By keeping a weekly master plan, you can make one grocery list and see to the shopping on the weekend—great for those who are used to catch-as-catch-can shopping on the way home from the office.

Keep 100 calories a day "free" for emergency eating.

When making up your daily menus, leave yourself this bit of room for leverage. Then if you find that one meal in particular didn't satisfy you, you have the calories for a small portion of food midway to your next meal to tide you over. The 100 calories could be saved for late in the evening as another option. Having this flexibility makes dieting a bit easier to master.

Diet wisely by choosing foods from all the major groups, albeit in smaller portions.

A diet must protect the physical integrity of your body; that means it should include the foods needed to sustain good health. Here are the minimum number of servings needed daily (portion sizes are in parentheses):

- **dairy**—2 servings; choose from low-fat milk (8 oz), cheese (1 oz), yogurt (4 oz), cottage cheese (4 oz)
- **meat/or seafood**—2 servings; lean meats (3 oz), poultry (4 oz), fish and shellfish (6 oz)
- **grains**—3 servings; (1 oz each) bread, rice, pasta
- **vegetables and fruits**—6 servings; (4 oz each) any variety
- **fats**—1 serving; (1 tbsp) butter, oil, salad dressing/ or mayonnaise, and similar products.

Make protein portions 15–20% of your daily caloric intake.

TIP #13

Protein is essential for cell repair and rejuvenation. If you deny yourself foods that supply protein, your body will draw it from its own organs and muscles, impairing good health. Yet not all protein sources are equally nutritious; choose your servings carefully, as suggested here:

- **as often as possible**: fish, chicken, and turkey (without the skin);
- **at least once a week**: chicken or calf's liver;
- **no more than twice a week**: eggs or shellfish (good sources of protein, but high in cholesterol), extra-lean beef, lamb, or pork;
- **avoid**: fatty meats, game, duck, goose.

Discover new varieties of fish, the preferred protein source.

TIP #14

Ounce for ounce, fish has the fewest calories of all protein sources—less than half those in beef, meaning you can double portion sizes! Here are just a few of the many different tastes available from the sea: bluefish, tuna, tilefish, monkfish, swordfish, shark. For a tasty and fast way to cook fillets, see tip #98.

Have protein-rich foods at breakfast.

Protein is often called brain food: It makes sense to fuel your mind as early in the day as possible. Try one of these choices:

- 99% fat-free cottage cheese (its high-protein, low-fat content makes it a great source);
- a protein shake of 1 egg, 8 oz of 99% fat-free milk, 4 oz any fruit, and 3 ice cubes mixed in the blender;
- sliced lean ham instead of, not in addition to, eggs;
- smoked fish.

 Make carbohydrates 55-65% of your daily caloric intake.

Take a tip from savvy marathon runners and become a carbohydrate overloader—the next time you feel like binging, eat all the green-and-yellow vegetables you can find! Note that beans, peas, and lentils are excellent sources, too, but have a high calorie count and should be eaten in small (1-ounce, cooked weight) portions.

 Include many complex carbohydrates in your diet: breads, potatoes, and rice.

Traditionally thought of as taboo, these are excellent staples that fill you up at a low-calorie cost. Make room for them by reducing the size of your protein/fat portions. Use this chart as a guide:

Have 3 oz of chicken and an 8 oz baked potato
instead of 5 oz of chicken;
2 oz of roast beef on a 2-oz crusty roll instead
of 5 oz of beef;
3 oz of sliced lamb and 4 oz of rice instead of
5 oz of lamb.

Make milk part of your diet plan.

TIP
#18

Tasty 99% fat-free milk supplies you with vital
nutrients —carbohydrates, protein, and vitamins A and
D—for good health and, when prepared as follows, can
replace your "comfort foods" when you're blue and need
soothing. Heat one cup of 99% fat-free milk to just before
a boil. Add a dash of nutmeg, ¼ teaspoon vanilla extract,
and a stick of cinnamon. Pour into a mug and sip. Calories:
100. Note: Heating milk makes it digestible to those whose
stomachs do not tolerate it well cold.

Start every day with orange juice.

TIP
#19

An excellent and low-calorie source of carbohydrates, vitamins, and minerals, o.j. is a great eye-opener.
To get the most nutrients, squeeze your own oranges on
a juicer. One-half cup has 55 calories.

TIP #20

Pasta is an ideal diet food.

Surprised? Don't be. It is a complex carbohydrate supplying you with vital nutrients, including B-complex vitamins. The secret to enjoying pasta is learning to gauge a moderate portion size and swearing off high-cal sauces. Using your kitchen scale (see tip #86), measure 3 ounces of any pasta product, dry. Cook as directed, then use your measuring cup to see the cooked volume of 3 ounces. Transfer to a dinner plate and notice how much surface is covered by the pasta. This is the ideal serving amount to consume. And once you can gauge it without your tools, you can enjoy it in restaurants (in a simple red tomato sauce; calorie count = 400).

TIP #21

Make fats 15–20% of your daily caloric intake.

Fats do play an important role in good health: They aid in the body's absorption of fat-soluble vitamins A, D, and E, and they help keep skin soft and hair shiny. Dieters agree that fats make low-calorie meals more palatable— better to have a small portion of tuna and some mayonnaise than a larger portion "dry." The healthier fats include cold-pressed vegetable oils (this process preserves more nutrients), such as sunflower, safflower, and olive oil.

While dieting, eliminate fatty meat products.

TIP #22

Frankfurters, bacon, salami, and sausages are really fat, not protein, items and offer few nutrients to boot. What they do contain are dangerous preservatives such as nitrites and nitrates (potentially cancer causing) and plenty of "artificials"—flavorings, colorings, and the like. Plan your menus around better foods than these for healthy weight loss.

 # Avoid margarine and butter "substitutes."

TIP #23

These low-calorie diet aids are often wasted calories: little of the taste and even less of the nutrients of the real thing. Because animal fats (butter and cream) are high in cholesterol, choose them infrequently to satisfy your fat portions, more as a treat then a daily habit.

 # Compensate for a reduced calorie and nutrient diet with vitamin supplements.

TIP #24

Make individual vitamin tablets your new strategy—an all-in-one pill simply isn't enough for you now. Begin with a 500-mg vitamin C tablet, a 50-mg B-complex capsule, a vitamin A and D tablet with 5,000 and 400 units respectively, and a 100-unit vitamin E capsule; work up from there. *You should consult your physician before taking vitamin and mineral supplements.*

Take a separate mineral supplement daily to boost the amount you are getting from your daily diet.

TIP #25

Minerals play an important role in good health—and in activating the fat-burning processes the body uses when on a diet. Minerals regulate the body's fluid balance, nerve and muscle function and often work in concert with vitamins, such as calcium and vitamin D in healthy bone and tooth formation. Leafy vegetables, "earth" vegetables such as onions and carrots, seafood and liver are excellent sources, but while on a restricted intake, have a daily supplement that includes potassium, calcium, iron, manganese, phosphorus, copper, and zinc.

 Drink 8 to 10 glasses of water every day.

TIP #26

Water is a natural appetite suppressant, flushes waste products out of your system, and keeps skin and hair healthy. Have a glass before and another during each meal, and you've already accounted for 6! Note: If your tap tastes terrible and bottled water is too rich for your budget, buy a water purifier that screws onto your faucet.

Always check with your doctor before starting a new diet.

TIP #27

The most important reason for this is to enable you and your physician to tailor the specific regimen to any particular health needs you have. If, for example, you have hypertension, a diet that recommends foods with a high sodium content might not be right for you. In addition to getting your physician's go-ahead, consider consulting a nutritionist to help you map out a plan for good health as well as for thinness.

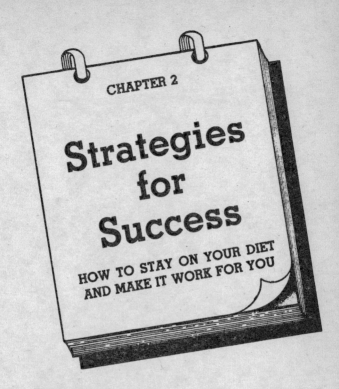

CHAPTER 2

Strategies for Success

HOW TO STAY ON YOUR DIET AND MAKE IT WORK FOR YOU

The key to staying on a diet is behavior modification—changing the eating patterns that led to your weight gain. You need to relearn how to deal with food, how to structure your day with less emphasis on eating, how to refocus your attention when the urge to eat between meals hits, and, when it is mealtime, how to enjoy your reduced portions most fully. These tips are targeted to meet each of these goals.

If you have a hard time staying on a diet for even 1 week, diet by the day.

TIP #28

Each morning, promise yourself that you'll stick with it all that day and night—take responsibility for a short 24-hour period. The following morning, acknowledge the previous day's success and repeat your promise. Challenging yourself on a daily basis is not as overwhelming as for a month or even 1 week. Each successive morning the promise gets easier to make and to keep, and before you know it, you will have chalked up 7 days. That feeling of accomplishment will give you the encouragement to help you through the second week.

TIP #29 **Make eating an activity unto itself, not something you do while reading, watching TV, or talking on the phone.**

If your mind is occupied by another activity, you simply won't feel as satisfied (or quite possibly satisfied *at all*) as if you had concentrated on your meal. Eating is as visual as it is oral: Keep your eyes on your food and you'll appreciate it much more.

TIP #30 **Eat when you are hungry.**

It is important to stick to the schedule you've outlined for your diet meals—miss one, and you'll be more than tempted to make up for it! So don't force yourself to wait until your spouse, kids, or roommate wants to eat; satisfy your hunger when you need to. If you would like to sit down with other household members when they do assemble, have a glass of juice or a cup of low-calorie consommé—it's the being together, not the food that counts!

Enjoy each and every meal you're entitled to.

TIP #31

Skipping meals just doesn't make good diet sense. Make a point of eating before excessive hunger sets in to prevent gorging later on. Eating a scheduled meal on time is doubly important when you know you'll be on the run. For example, never try to make it on breakfast alone when you have a full day of appointments or even shopping ahead of you—you'll either faint, hole up at the nearest soda fountain, or, if you last until dinner, spend the rest of the night pigging out! Conclusion: Stick to your daily menu plan.

 Prolong every meal to 20 minutes, the time it takes for your brain to acknowledge the food and send out the message that hunger is over.

TIP #32

Some delaying tactics:

- eating with chopsticks (works for every cuisine);
- eating corn kernels, peas, beans, and the like one by one;
- using your napkin after every bite;
- chewing each bite 8 times;
- drinking your beverage in sips;
- serving food too hot to eat quickly;
- serving foods that have to be cut and cutting off only one bite at a time.

TIP #33 **Eat your portions in 2 helpings.**

Start by placing half of each serving on your plate. Eat slowly (as though there were twice as much!). Then enjoy your "second helping." You aren't eating any more than you should; you're simply tricking your tummy into thinking you are.

TIP #34 **Keep your menus varied.**

Make a point of including 3 new foods in your meal plan each and every week. Consider a purée of parsnips instead of the usual green beans. Try bay scallops broiled with a dash of soy sauce instead of run-of-the-mill canned fish. Oval Italian tomatoes make a delicious change from the usual round variety and add bright color to your salad. Dieting doesn't have to be boring!

TIP #35 **Always have a menu contingency plan.**

Let's say you planned to buy a roasted chicken on your way home but worked too late to get to the butcher; knowing that you can instead pick up a ¼ pound of sliced turkey at the all-night deli will keep you from reaching for the nearest high-calorie convenience food.

If menu planning becomes impossible, pare down to one food basic.

After weeks of dieting, the energy that goes into creative meal planning can't always be sustained. Basing your intake on one key item, such as yogurt or cottage cheese, makes it easier to stick with dieting. Round out the single food with no-preparation staples, such as fruit, vegetables that can be eaten raw, and whole grain bread eaten as is or lightly toasted. Continue this effortless eating plan until you feel the need to return to more interesting meals— 1 week, 2 weeks, or perhaps not until you are ready for maintenance.

 Make a point of having breakfast before you go to work.

If you are in the habit of starting your day on an empty stomach, teach yourself how to eat in the morning, an important practice for good health and to avoid mid-morning diet hunger. Start with a small meal of juice and a piece of plain toast, the most simple, and easily consumed, choice. In a week, replace the toast with cereal, such as Kellogg's Nutri•Grain line, which does not contain sugar, and 4 ounces of 99% fat-free milk. Then progressively add 50 calories a week to this meal until you are eating a healthy 300 calories.

23

Allow yourself a special treat for breakfast—once a month!

A within-limits treat: a croissant, well heated to bring out its natural flavor without added butter (there's plenty in it already!), with just 1 teaspoon of preserves. A Sunday brunch alternative: the New York special—half a bagel (about 2 ounces), 1 ounce of cream cheese, and 2 ounces of any smoked fish. Calorie count of either choice = 400.

 Fend off office hunger pangs before lunch with a late morning mini-meal.

An ounce packet of almonds or sunflower seeds and 4 ounces of tomato juice will satisfy your needs; postpone lunch until 1 P.M. and be sure to cut back on that meal's calories (185) accordingly.

 Swear off foods readily available at the office.

One of our dieters, the assistant producer of a talk show, faces each new day with 3 dozen donuts that arrive for the guests and the crew to consume during the show's taping. Loving donuts, she was unable to stop with one. Her only choice was to tell herself that they were completely off-limits. If you can't consume in moderation, do without.

Keep a low-calorie mini-larder in your office to take care of your beverage needs.

Permissible edibles to store at work include diet sodas, packets of bouillon, powdered skim milk, and herbal teas. And having a special mug to drink from will give you a psychological boost.

 Take on new responsibilities at work.

Volunteer for a special project that will entail more hours and lots of energy. Your mind will automatically begin to redirect the effort it puts into thinking about food toward this new endeavor. As this helps you lose weight, you make important career gains!

 Postpone your dinner hour with appetite-cutting activity.

To avoid the home——boredom——binge cycle, get out of your food-motivated rut and pep up your social life at least 3 evenings a week. Start with a slight variation at first, a short walk or a 6 P.M. movie followed by a quick bite instead of a full meal. If you have a spouse who expects food on the table when he or she comes home, explain that these small adventures will spice up your relationship as they help diminish the importance food plays in your life.

Stop eating as soon as you feel full.

Sounds like obvious advice, but it is rarely followed by a food lover. Those of us with weight problems keep eating until the plate, if not the entire kitchen, is clean! To break this pattern, be more conscious of the way you feel after every bite of food. If you just shovel down every portion, you really don't give yourself time to realize: "Hey, I'm full already." But if you take the time, you will find that you are sated *before* every last morsel has been eaten. Note: When you are finished, clear your place at home or, in a restaurant, call for the waiter to take your dishes away; this keeps you from nibbling while others at your table finish.

When you have finished eating your last diet portion for the day, close the kitchen.

Wipe down the counters, run the dishwasher, turn out the lights, and close the door. This strong symbolic act says "no more food tonight," while a lit kitchen is a tempting open invitation.

TIP #46 | Look for low-cal ways to enjoy a love of food.

If you and your spouse's favorite pastime is canvasing your city for the best goat cheese and red wine, you're dedicated food lovers. Instead of trying to give up this shared passion, rechannel it into "dietetic" avenues. Plan an outing to an apple orchard or a strawberry farm where you can do your own picking—lots of fun, lots of exercise, and lots of low-cal (and low-priced) fruit to take home.

TIP #47 | Indulge in your favorite foods on occasion—it's allowed!

Total restriction spells failure: The more you suppress a craving, the greater the binge will be when you finally explode. To learn to control your urges as you diet, incorporate limited amounts of these favorites into your weekly meal plan—one, once a week. Note that the item is not in addition to your allotted diet portions but part of them. Not only does this technique satisfy your taste-buds, but it also helps you stick to your diet by getting rid of the denial factor that is so frustrating.

Save Sunday evening for your weekly indulgence.

TIP #48

Although you can apply the previous tip as you like best, saving your special food portion for the very end of the diet week can serve as week-long motivation to be "good." Conversely, indulging early in the week can disrupt you for the rest of the week; indulging early in the day can leave you wanting more and more. Being able to wait means you are learning the control that will keep you thin.

 All bites taste the same, so all you need is one!

TIP #49

Here's how to teach yourself to be satisfied with a single taste. Bake a cake and slice it into 7 portions. Freeze 6 of the pieces individually. Then take one forkful of the seventh slice and savor it slowly. Give the rest of this piece to someone else to finish or, if you are alone, throw it away. Repeat this exercise in self-control once a day until the cake is used up: Defrost it piece by piece in the A.M., sample it in the P.M. By being able to stop at one bite, you will break the overindulgence habit that caused you to gain in the first place.

TIP #50

To appease a massive craving, make tomorrow Chocolate Pudding Day.

Or Cookie Day. Or Egg Noodle Day. The situation: It's 3 P.M. and you are having a pudding fit. Since you've already eaten more than half of your calories for the day, decide to indulge your craving...tomorrow, when you have the calories to work with. The anticipation will be enough to get you through the rest of today. Tomorrow buy enough pudding mix to make 8 ½-cup servings (2 small boxes—1200 calories when made with 99% fat-free milk). Prepare the pudding and consume any way you'd like with this caution: This is all you can eat all day. At 1200 calories you will be sticking with your diet; you'll continue on your weight loss pattern; and you'll satisfy your pudding (or whatever your chosen food is) craving for the year! The next day, simply resume your week's diet menu plan. Why can't you do this every day? Because it is an unsound way of eating for the long term and your diet should help you not only to lose weight but to improve your health as well.

TIP #51

Brand your overindulgences in your diet journal with a scarlet letter.

If you find it impossible to resist eating an extra portion, then add the item to your journal (see tip #9) in red. This is a psychological tool: It acts as a reminder of your over-indulgence and will prompt you to try harder tomorrow. In fact, very often just knowing that you will be writing in the entry in red will be the straw needed to break the temptation and keep you on track.

Always carry your calorie counter book with you, even if you think you know the content of most foods.

(See tip #4.) In the event that you are tempted by a new item on a menu, you'll be prepared to look it up and know one way or another if it falls into your limit and how much of it you can have.

 When you can't calculate the calories in a dish exactly, estimate high, at 200 calories an ounce.

That is the average calorie count of butter, mayonnaise, and most oils, the most calorie-dense foods—the maximum an ounce serving of any dish could be. Chances are most dishes will fall short of this count, but to keep yourself from overeating, use it as your mathematical rule when in doubt.

 To take your mind off your hunger when a meal is delayed, always carry a paperback with you.

One of our dieters keeps a copy of her favorite author's latest work in her shoulder bag. She whips it out and quiets her appetite whenever she's sitting at the lunch counter of her nearby diner waiting for her fish order to be cooked to her liking; when her veal roast dinner needs another 15 minutes in the oven; when her date gets caught in traffic on his way to her place. Try it—it will work for you, too.

Clean out your closets!

TIP #55   The next time a munch attack is imminent, go to work—you'll stay busy for hours, and your accomplishment will leave you feeling even more satisfied than had you downed a vanilla float!

Put an end to all habits you associate with snacking.

TIP #56

If you can't watch TV without a bowl of nuts, stop watching TV. If you can't read a book without nibbling on crackers, stop reading. After about a day or two of this kind of deprivation, you'll probably realize that you're going to have to rethink the way you live—to a person who loves eating, almost everything can be associated with food! The solution then is to change the way you conduct your activities. Example: If the TV is in the living room, move it into the laundry room and do your ironing as you watch. If you're used to reading in bed, try reading in the living room or as you soak in the bathtub. Do not do any kind of eating in these new settings to be sure that these new habits stay unassociated with food.

If nighttime eating is your problem, devise an hour-by-hour strategy to get you from dinner to bedtime.

TIP
#57

Example:

7 P.M.: write a letter to Mom and Dad;
8 P.M.: take a French lesson on the home
          computer;
9 P.M.: prepare clothes for tomorrow morning,
          touch up nail polish (for women), or
          shave (for men);
10 P.M.: walk the dog and get the early edition of
          tomorrow's paper; read until sleepy.

 Break the habit of scheduling your day around the meal clock.

TIP
#58

Overweight people are inclined to live from one meal to the next rather than from one activity to the next. Thin people eat when it accommodates their schedule, not the other way around. Think thin.

Renew your interest in staying on your diet by varying your weight loss program every 3 months.

Try switching from a calorie-counting diet to one that tracks "portions." Or to a high-carbohydrate diet. Or to a modified vegetarian plan—swear off meat but include eggs, cheese, fish, and chicken. Learning the specifics of a new diet added to the anticipation of a change in routine helps break the monotony that so often leads dieters astray.

 ## Keep your diet out of the headlines!

Avoid telling everyone you know that you are dieting. It's hard enough to get from one meal to the next without having the added annoyance of well-meaning friends bombarding you with questions about your progress. Truth be told, after a while you would end up boring everyone, yourself included, to tears.

 ## Plan social get-togethers that revolve around activity rather than eating.

Instead of inviting your favorite couple to dinner, make an after-8 date for cards, bridge, or perhaps Trivial Pursuit, the popular board game. (If you must serve something, make it fresh fruit or a fruit sorbet, ices made with a minimum of sugar.) Use your imagination, and you will uncover many pleasing diversions that don't include food. Remember museums? Art galleries? The park? Sure you do!

TIP #62 | **Be the life of every party.**

The more amusing you are, the more attention you'll get and the less attention you'll want to pay to food and drink. This will take practice if you're usually the attentive listener in the group, but it's all part of your needed life-style change.

TIP #63 | **Make mineral water your "usual" drink.**

Domestic or imported carbonated waters, club soda, or seltzer, this no-calorie refresher is a great no-chemical replacement for diet sodas and the like. With a squeeze of lemon or lime, soda water is an excellent appetite suppressant. And always have an extra 6-pack or 2 in the fridge: Pack a chilled can in your bag or tote to have anytime, anywhere you need it.

TIP #64 | **Steer clear of finger foods.**

They find their way to your mouth too easily. Using a knife and fork prolongs the pleasure and gives your brain more time to register the meal and turn off its hunger alert!

TIP #65 ## Work to curb a sugar addiction.

Yes, sugar can be very addictive. Eating one cookie isn't the problem; it's not being able to stop with one cookie. Sugar always leaves you wanting more, more per serving, more servings overall. Because it's a refined food, the carbohydrates in sugar aren't as valuable as natural carb sources. That combined with the high-cal count of most sugar-based products is why sugar has no place in a diet: When you must limit calories, you need to consume those with the highest nutrients. Cut back *gradually* to reduce the occurrence of "sugar blues," the depressed side effect of going off sugar, but steadily to help promote weight loss and keep your stamina high.

TIP #66 ## Drink caffeinated beverages with caution if you use them to curb between-meal cravings.

Because of their no-calorie count, coffee or tea is suggested on every diet plan. But because of their caffeine content, they tend to make dieters very jumpy—and just being on a diet makes you jumpy enough. So try to limit your dependency on them. Note: To help make up for the sacrifice of cream and sugar, when you must have a cup, use a tablespoon of whole milk to give tea or coffee "body" and to make it more satisfying (calorie count = 10).

Accept the fact that drinking and dieting don't mix.

TIP #67

Extra weight can often be due to an overindulgence in liquor rather than in food. A glass of wine with lunch, a cocktail to unwind after work, another glass or two of wine with dinner—these are calories that add up. To diet successfully, limit yourself to 1 drink a week, adjusting that day's calorie count accordingly. Note that lite beers and wine spritzers go nearly twice as far as ordinary drinks.

white wine spritzer (1½ oz wine, 4 oz club soda)	=	38 calories
white wine, 3 oz	=	75 calories
red wine, 3 oz	=	90 calories
champagne, 3 oz	=	75 calories
cognac, 1 oz	=	100 calories
rum, vodka, whiskey, 1 oz, 80 proof	=	65 calories
gin, scotch, 1 oz, 94 proof	=	75 calories
beer, 12 oz	=	160 calories
lite beer, 12 oz	=	90 calories
gin and tonic, 1 jigger to 6 oz tonic	=	170 calories
bloody mary, 1 jigger vodka to 6 oz tomato juice	=	135 calories

CHAPTER 3

At the Market

SHOPPING WISELY

For most dieters the problem of managing food begins at the supermarket—once forbidden items are in your shopping cart, they're as good as eaten! By relearning the fine art of food shopping—making changes in how and where you buy food—you can increase your weight loss success. The following tips show you how to clue into labels, how to choose properly, and which new products merit a try.

☐ TIP #68 | Always shop from a careful list.

Before going to the supermarket, prepare a list of items you'll need for a full week and buy only those items. The less you are exposed to the tempting foods on grocery shelves, the easier it will be to stay on your diet.

☐ TIP #69 | Shop on a full stomach to keep from nibbling your way down the food aisles.

Everyone has, at one time or another, opened a box of cookies out of hunger and wound up paying for the empty container at the checkout line! Naturally, this is a diet disaster; going shopping *after* a meal means you can get through the store easily and without going off your list. And for those who shop on the way home, after work and before dinner, the food to nibble is 8 ounces of grapes (calorie count = 100); they make a satisfying "appetizer" that falls within your diet plan.

When food shopping, think small.

TIP #70 When faced with a size choice, always go for the smallest option: thin-sliced bread, not sandwich size; small eggs, not medium or large; 4-ounce and 6-ounce containers of yogurt or cottage cheese, not 8-ounce or 16-ounce. This will help you streamline your portions to slim-person size!

Get the most nutrients for your calories by shopping a greengrocer.

TIP #71

This is particularly important when buying fresh produce, the fruits and vegetables that provide most of the bulk of diet meals. Greengrocers have the freshest food, which you can select and bag yourself. And since you can choose the exact amounts you need, there won't be any "leftover" opportunities to overeat.

Investigate gourmet food shops for low-calorie splurges.

TIP #72

Berries otherwise out of season, exotic flavors of vinegar to liven up salads, wild mushrooms the likes of which aren't available at the average grocery—these are some of the allowed foods that you can treat yourself to on special occasions, to make dieting a bit more fun. But do limit these shopping excursions to once a month, because your local gourmet shop will also feature items like triple fudge sauce, something you shouldn't expose yourself to very often!

▢ TIP #73   **Become a label reader.**

Getting into this habit is vital if you rely on packaged foods. All diet products are required to list calorie counts; many other products list them voluntarily. The most important fact to check is the number of calories per serving and the serving size. A package of mixed vegetables might say "50 calories a serving"—fine if the serving is 1 cup and leaves you satisfied, not so fine if it's ½-cup that leaves you wanting more. If a product label doesn't list its calories, don't buy it—it could lead you off your diet!

▢ TIP #74   **Become a comparison shopper.**

Not all "diet" foods are created equal: Calorie counts vary. Ovaltine Hot Chocolate Mix, for example, is made with NutraSweet and contains only 40 calories per serving; most other diet brands check in at 70. By the same token, not all regular foods are created equal: Contadina tomato paste, unlike most other brands, contains no sugar and can be considered a good food for the dieter. The more you compare, the more value you get for your calories and the more satisfied a dieter you will be.

Never take the contents of any food for granted.

TIP #75

Read the ingredients on every food label and be aware of hidden calories. The words *glucose, lactose*, and *fructose* all mean one thing—added sugar—and can be found in items you'd never suspect, from canned peas to chicken franks! Know what you're getting in the way of nutrition or put the item back on the shelf.

 Choose typical diet foods only if they satisfy your tastes.

TIP #76

Yes, cottage cheese, celery, and carrots are the mainstays of many diets, but you needn't limit yourself to them or include them at all if you don't genuinely like them. There are other low-cal veggies and products that are good tasting: try cauliflower buds and cucumber spears, fruited yogurts or tofu products. Remember, diet means moderation, not deprivation. Keep your food options open, and losing weight will be less of a sacrifice.

 Research new diet aids that come on the market.

TIP #77

Some skeptics think that something new can't be any good—that philosophy could cost you calories! One of the best diet aids is the newly developed low-cal sweetener Equal®, a product without saccharin and its aftertaste. Each packet is equivalent to two teaspoons of sugar, with only 4 calories. Also look for it as an ingredient in other products such as NutraSweet.

TIP #78

Buy a cooking oil spray instead of the usual bottled varieties.

PAM® is a very useful diet aid that contains a propellant to spray a very small amount of vegetable oil on the surface of your pans, eliminating the need for tablespoons of oil or butter. Each spray has only 7 calories and 1 gram of fat. In addition to the vegetable oil and the propellant, there is a small amount of alcohol and lecithin, a vegetable compound. You will need to practice using PAM to control the amount you spray, but this is one product well worth trying.

TIP #79

For a change in low-calorie beverages, try sugar-free powdered drink mixes.

Lemonade, pink lemonade, and fruit punch are just 3 of the flavors available in handy-to-store containers. Just mix with water and add ice—only-4-calories-to-a-cup refreshment! NutraSweet and natural flavors work the magic. Country Time, Crystal Light, and Wyler's are three brands to try.

**Pep up salads—a dieting staple—
with new varieties of lettuce.**

TIP #80

Did you know that you could eat 2 pounds of lettuce (16 cups!) for fewer than a hundred calories? Problem is, the run-of-the-mill iceberg has little pizzazz (and the fewest nutrients of any variety, too). Jazz up your home salad bowl with these new looks in lettuce: romaine, loose-leaf, red leaf, endive, Boston, butterhead, Bibb, curly leaf, and the Italian maroon-colored raddicchio.

 **Buy a wide variety of diet
dressings and experiment with
them on non-salad dishes.**

TIP #81

Low-calorie dressings are a boon to the dieter but aren't for salads only. Try diet Italian over sliced chicken, diet French on lean roast beef or cold shrimp, diet Russian instead of mayonnaise on shredded cabbage for low-cal cole slaw.

TIP #82

Select frozen diet dinners with caution.

These are great convenience items, as all your courses are in one package. However, the brand you buy should not exceed 300 calories; if it does, you're not getting good value—those that total closer to 500 calories give you too much to consume at any one meal and certainly at night. To compensate for the smaller, lower calorie portions, add a piece of fresh fruit to the meal. Note: A great alternative to the frozen dinner is a meal-in-a-can soup, such as Campbell's Chunky Soup, that can be heated in 5 minutes, a fraction of the time it takes to cook the other.

TIP #83

Be aware of food additives.

If you are under a physician's care, you will know whether you need to avoid products with salt or cholesterol, for instance. But there are other additives you might not realize aren't very beneficial. Artificial colorings, flavorings, and preservatives found in frozen, canned, and boxed foods do little to provide you with good health. While you are dieting, you need even more nutrients than usual, so try to avoid foods that contribute little more than chemicals.

CHAPTER 4

Eating In

A NEW APPROACH TO FOOD

Reorganizing your kitchen and your style of cooking are musts for successful dieting—if not, you face temptation every time you open the fridge. The tips in this chapter show you how to make the most of your portions, helping you stay on your diet whether you're eating alone or entertaining a large group. And remember that all our recipes passed our own discriminating (and weight-conscious!) palates.

Clean out your kitchen to help insure success.

TIP
#84

One of our most recent successful dieters admits she spent 3 years on the yo-yo system, losing and gaining back the same 50 pounds because she didn't approach dieting with a fervor. The fervor must begin in your kitchen, where everything that doesn't conform to your diet must be thrown out. That includes canned goods and items in the freezer—during a previous attempt, this dieter thought she could resist frozen almond cookies. She not only craved them, she found she could thaw them in her mouth! Make a clean sweep of forbidden foods and then restock according to your specific diet's guidelines and the suggestions in tips #85 and #89.

Put the contents of your refrigerator on a diet.

TIP #85

In addition to the items required for your daily menus, keep only a few key diet aids in the fridge:

- lemons and limes, excellent flavoring agents;
- sugar-free cereals and grain products, such as breadsticks and whole wheat crackers of fewer than 20 calories each;
- a few servings of diet gelatin (try Jell-O's new brand made with NutraSweet®—only 8 calories!);
- tuna packed in water—tastes best cold;
- low-calorie mayonnaise substitute, such as Kraft's new Miracle Whip *Light*—40 calories a tablespoon;
- low-calorie vegetable juices, such as tomato and V-8.

 Invest in a high-quality kitchen scale to calculate calories most accurately.

TIP #86

Weigh each and every portion you dole out and, using your calorie book (see tip #4), mark down its calorie count to keep track of your intake. The newest scales are computerized; many, such as Compucal's Diet/Kitchen Computer, have memory banks that calculate the calories for you at the push of a button. These make the old mini-postal scales obsolete!

TIP #87 **Use your kitchen scale to help you learn to gauge portion sizes when eating out.**

Place a measuring cup on your scale (see tip #86) and reset the indicator to 0 to negate its weight. Fill the cup with 1 ounce of dry cereal, then pour the cereal in a bowl. Note the size of the mass, how far up the sides the cereal reaches, how much of the bowl is covered. Now test yourself by pouring the cereal back into the box and then refill the bowl directly from it. Pour the cereal into the measuring cup and weigh it to see how close you came to 1 ounce. Practice every morning until you can pour an ounce of cereal without your measuring tools. Note: You can learn to gauge every food that can be measured in a cup this way. Repeat the exercise with berries, sliced carrots, and raisins. Expand your repertoire as you become more proficient: Once you can calculate portions, you can control your weight *forever*.

TIP #88 **Learn to gauge the portion size of meats.**

Roast a chicken, turkey, leg of lamb, or other lean cut of meat. Slice and measure 4 ounces on your scale (see tip #86). Place the slices on a standard dinner plate. Note how much surface the slices cover. Test yourself by slicing your estimate of 4 ounces, then weigh and correct the portion as needed. By the time you've carved your roast, you'll know exactly what 4 ounces looks like!

TIP #89

Spice up your diet recipes with low-cal enhancers.

Your tastebuds can always be satisfied if you use these ingredients to flavor your meals:

- spices, all varieties including cinnamon, nutmeg, saffron, curry;
- herbs, all varieties including oregano, chervil, parsley, basil;
- vinegars, all varieties including balsamic, sherry, tarragon, berry, red wine, and cider-based;
- bouillon, in cube or powder, in beef, chicken, and vegetable flavors to add to sauces, cooking juices, marinades;
- low-cal "sauces" such as soy, tamara, and Worcestershire.

TIP #90

Make versatile mustard your preferred low-calorie condiment.

French-style white wine mustards, such as dijon, can add zest to dishes such as broiled veal chops (sprinkle on herbs before cooking, too). Green peppercorn mustard gives low-calorie salad dressing a lift. Spicy brown mustard, thinned with water and a dollop of diet mayonnaise, makes a great spread for cold cuts. If you've been relying on plain yellow mustard, you (and your diet) will be pleasantly surprised by the change.

Take the sweets out of your home sweet home.

TIP #91

If you aren't able to restrict your intake of cakes, cookies, etc., don't keep them in your kitchen. Indulge only in restaurants and ask for half-portions to keep calories down.

 Get the most from your calories by choosing high-volume foods.

TIP #92

When deciding how to use up a 300-calorie allotment, for instance, consider the "fill-up" value of the foods you are considering. Certainly the idea of 6 Oreo cookies is tempting, but half a roast chicken (without the skin) will fill you up—the cookies will leave you wanting more. You would get even more from a quarter of a roast chicken and a huge green leaf salad. Be sure you determine how to get the most for your calories before you reach for food, and you won't have to deal with hunger very often.

Eat your meals in as many courses as possible.

TIP #93

This gives the illusion of eating more, and the food takes more time to consume. For example, at breakfast, instead of reaching for a plain muffin, have 1 cup of berries, followed by one slice of thin, whole wheat toast and herbal tea, and finally an egg-white omelette (great for dieters who are also cholesterol conscious).

THREE-EGG-WHITE OMELETTE

Ingredients: 3 eggs
PAM® cooking spray
herbs, such as thyme and oregano

Separate the eggs and discard the high-cal yolks. Beat the whites lightly with a whisk. Spray your fry pan with PAM® and heat it. Pour in the eggs, sprinkle on herbs, and fold in half as you would with a regular omelette. Turn once to cook evenly.
Makes 1 serving; calorie count = 45 (with blueberries and toast, 180).

If you're going to be working late, have dinner waiting for you at home.

Having a long stretch between lunch and dinner will make you want to grab the first thing you see in the fridge, so plan ahead and have a made-that-morning meal already there or pick up a ready-made entrée at a food shop on your way home. Your hunger won't allow you to start fussing with elaborate preparations; be able to satisfy it quickly. Here are some choices:

- A Sunday night roast makes easy-to-slice sandwich filling midweek;
- section fruit in the A.M. to ring a mound of cottage cheese in the P.M.;
- steam assorted veggies the night before and toss with diet dressing just before eating.

 When you make a multiple-serving recipe, divide the portions immediately.

This helps you avoid cheating on portions later on—that's when 4 quarter-portions turn into one-half, one-third, a few remaining forkfuls, and a missed meal! Be sure to identify each serving with the following information: the item, its calorie count, the date and time of the meal it is intended for. If the dish is for you alone, add your name and a polite hands-off warning to the nondieters in your house.

TIP #96

Use opaque plastic containers to store do-ahead meals and leftovers.

It's easier to resist temptation if you can't see the inviting foods every time you open the fridge for a club soda!

TIP #97

Always remove all visible fat before preparing meat or poultry parts.

For beef and other meats, a boning knife does an excellent job. The "fat" of a chicken or turkey is the skin and those yellow deposits found underneath it. When cooking chicken or turkey pieces, it is much better to remove the skin and the bones with your knife prior to cooking; but when roasting whole fowl, leave the skin on during cooking to preserve natural moistness, then remove and discard before you are tempted to nibble.

TIP #98 **Try broiling foods for a natural flavor without the calories of an added sauce.**

Broiling is fast and delicious, especially when you use an outdoor grill to which flavor chips, such as mesquite, have been added. Broiling is a convenience for the indoor cook as well—it takes half the time to broil a chicken cutlet than it does to bake one! Fish is a favorite for broiling— no messy odors or cleanup, especially when you use fillets. Try this delicious Japanese-style "steak" recipe.

SALMON TERIYAKI

Ingredients: 4 oz salmon steak
1 tsp honey
1 tsp soy sauce
1 scallion, finely chopped

Mix the honey, the soy sauce, and the scallion. Spread on the salmon steak. Place under your oven broiler for 10 minutes; do not turn. Makes 1 serving; calorie count = 230.

For fast, no-added-calorie cooking, buy a stainless steel steamer.

TIP #99

For \$5, you can have a utensil that fits inside nearly every pan, expanding to accommodate each individual pan's diameter. In 10 minutes you can steam a pound of string beans, for example, preserving the nutrients boiling removes. Simply place 2 inches of water in your pan, bring to a boil, add the steamer filled with the food to be cooked, turn the heat down to simmer, and cover. The Chinese steam everything from vegetables to buns; here's a low-calorie version of Oriental steamed meatballs.

PEARL BALLS

Ingredients:
    1 lb. finely ground chicken (raw)
    1 small egg
    1 tsp salt
    1 tbsp soy sauce
    1 tbsp cornstarch
    1 oz water chestnuts, finely chopped
    1 scallion, finely chopped

Mix the cornstarch with two tablespoons of water and combine with the rest of the ingredients. Open your steamer and spray it with PAM (see tip #78). Roll the mixture into 30 balls and place them on the steamer, separating them by ½ inch. Using a saucepan wide enough to accommodate the steamer, fill with 2 inches of water and bring to boil. Place the steamer inside and cover. Turn the heat down to a simmer and cook for 20 minutes. Makes 4 servings; calorie count = 235.

TIP #100

To start your day with a well-nourished (and low-cal!) feeling, rediscover childhood breakfast foods.

Hot cereals, such as Cream of Wheat and Cream of Rice, offer an added boost of iron (vital to women on a diet) and, when made with 99% fat-free milk instead of water, provide needed calcium. Garnish the 1-cup, 230-calorie serving the adult way, with one teaspoon of honey and two of crushed nuts; calorie count = 290.

TIP #101

For variety, replace the old apple-a-day adage with a banana.

One hundred calories of energy, potassium, and a sweet kick that's good for you. As an alternative to eating it straight, try a banana shake—great at breakfast or as a snack.

BANANA SMOOTHIE

Ingredients: 1 banana
4 oz 99% fat-free milk
3 ice cubes
a pinch each of cinnamon and
nutmeg

Place all the ingredients in a blender and process until smooth, about 30 seconds.
Calorie count = 150.

TIP #102

For a different eating adventure any time of the day, try the new French custard-style yogurts.

A 6-oz cup has 200 calories (the same as ordinary flavored yogurts), yet is so much creamier that you feel like you're eating dessert—a boon to the sweet tooth with less sugar than a real custard and lots more nutrients. The best part? The exotic flavors: piña colada, tropical fruit, strawberry-banana!

TIP #103

Create a low-cal "sandwich" by using large leaf lettuce and other adaptable veggies to hold your filling.

Two treats to try:

1. Romaine roll-ups. Place two outer leaves of a head of romaine lettuce on a plate. Sprinkle on each 1 ounce alfalfa sprouts, 1 ounce shredded cheese or chicken. Starting at the top of a leaf, roll up the "sandwich" into a compact tube shape; repeat with the other leaf. Makes 1 serving; calorie count = 220 if made with cheese, 120 if made with chicken. (May be made up to 2 hours in advance without wilting.)

2. Cucumber boats. Slice an unpeeled cucumber lengthwise and use a grapefruit knife to remove the seeds. In each half, place 2 ounces of tuna. Drizzle on a tablespoon of plain yogurt mixed with a dash of curry powder and top with 4 cherry tomato halves. Makes 1 serving; calorie count = 160. (May be made a day in advance.)

TIP #104

Use tomatoes to sauce your favorite dishes.

Try this tastes-great-on-everything tomato sauce the next time you want to dress up chicken cutlets, pasta, seafood, even string beans!

FAST AND EASY TOMATO SAUCE

Ingredients:
1 clove of garlic, peeled and chopped
½ tbsp of olive or safflower oil
¼ cup chopped fresh parsley
1 chopped onion
1 chopped green pepper
1 28-oz can of crushed, peeled tomatoes

Sauté the garlic in the oil for 3 minutes, then add the onion and cook until translucent. Add the green pepper and the parsley. Stir frequently for 5 minutes, then add the can of tomatoes with its juice. Heat thoroughly. Add ¼ to ½ cup of water if the sauce is too thick. Simmer for 10 minutes.

Makes 6–7 ½-cup servings; calorie count = 60.

Variation: Use 8 ounces chopped fresh mushrooms instead of the onion and green pepper.

TIP #105

Make the often-overlooked cabbage one of your diet staples.

Cabbage is both extremely low in calories (24 per cup) and very adaptable. Consider these uses for one head: The large outer leaves are perfect for stuffed cabbage made with ground chicken or veal; steamed cabbage slices make a good accompaniment to lean corned beef; grated cabbage adds zest to salads; cole slaw and sauerkraut make tasty side dishes.

TIP #106

Use whole potatoes to create fabulous (and low-calorie) one-dish meals.

Potatoes are undeservedly put on most diets' lists of no-nos. They are packed with B-complex vitamins and important minerals, such as potassium. Many fast-food restaurants have introduced the potato-plus-topping dish as an alternative to burgers and fried-food sandwiches. At home, you can make even more exciting combinations. To get all the nutrients in this low-cal package, be sure to eat your potatoes whole, skin and all. Here are some "stuffing" ideas:

- flaked smoked salmon in a yogurt-and-dill dressing;
- ham and cheddar cheese cubes;
- sautéed mushrooms and onions;
- ricotta cheese and chopped walnuts.

TIP #107 **If you're bored with raw vegetable nibbles, juice them!**

This is an excellent way to get more liquids into your system and to give your diet a lift. A juice extractor works equally well on noncitrus fruits, such as apples and pears. To preserve some of the fibrous pulp (rich in vitamins) that juicing normally removes, don't use the extrafine filter that comes with most of these appliances.

 TIP #108 **Avoid making high-calorie recipes while on a diet.**

Even if you're cooking for others—the kids, the church bake sale, or the neighbors' potluck supper—create a low-cal alternative or buy something already made. That's the only way you'll avoid being tempted to lick the bowl! Homemade might be best, but try to think of yourself first...at least this once.

TIP #109

For the nonchef: Prepare minimal-cooking meals.

There are many quick-cook or no-cook menus that are appetizing and easy, making it possible to control your intake without worrying about restaurant-sized portions. Here are some options:

- mixed green salad with cheese cubes and alfalfa sprouts;
- frozen yogurt with melon cubes, walnut bits, and raisins;
- cold sliced chicken and broccoli flowerettes;
- diced ham, cherry tomatoes, and red onion rings;
- tuna and artichoke hearts on endive.

TIP #110

Make your diet meals as pleasing to the eye as to the palate.

The presentation of food is most important, especially when you're sacrificing calories—visual appeal makes up for smaller portions. Take the time to make your plate as appetizing as possible, with radish rosettes, tomato "flowers," a bouquet of watercress wrapped with a red-pepper-strip bow. For more elaborate embellishments, shop the cooking section of your favorite bookstore for a volume on this delicate and tasty art.

To add variety to your diet, try one new vegetable each week.

TIP #111

To properly introduce it to your tastebuds, find 3 different recipes to try as well. If as a child you hated spinach, for instance, now is the time to sample spinach-and-mushroom salad, poached eggs florentine, and spinach soufflé.

SPINACH SOUFFLÉ

Ingredients:
- ¼ cup flour
- 1 cup of whole milk
- 1 lb spinach leaves, washed as directed below, then steamed and chopped
- 1 small onion, chopped and steamed
- 2 oz Swiss cheese, shredded
- 6 eggs, separated
- nutmeg and black pepper
- ⅛ tsp cream of tartar

To wash the spinach leaves, soak them in a large pot or bowl of cold water for 10 minutes. Shake the leaves gently, allowing the grit to settle to the bottom of the receptacle. Lift out each leaf and discard the water. Repeat the process, then drain the leaves before steaming (see tip #99). Chop the cooked spinach until fine and set aside. In a saucepan, blend the flour and milk and cook until thick, about 3 minutes. Remove from heat. Add the chopped spinach and onion and a pinch each of nutmeg and black pepper to the milk-flour mixture. Then stir in the cheese and the egg yolks, one at a time. In a large bowl, beat the egg whites gently, then add the cream of tartar and continue beating until they hold a firm shape. Gently fold the whites into the spinach mixture and pour into a 1½-quart soufflé dish that has been sprayed with PAM (see tip #78). Bake in a preheated oven at 375 degrees for 30 minutes. Makes 4 servings; calorie count = 250.

TIP #112

Pamper your tastebuds with mail-order delicacies that fit into your diet.

Smoked turkey from upstate New York, cheddar cheese from the source in Wisconsin, and live lobsters from Maine are just three possibilities to rouse you from diet doldrums. Check the back pages of food and shelter magazines for mail-order companies—many offer toll-free numbers and delivery within one week. These aren't everyday splurges, but chosen once a month or even every other month, they can renew your dieting incentive.

TIP #113

Subscribe to *Food & Wine* magazine for a delightful change from diet-food periodicals.

In addition to highlighting a wide variety of cuisines, the magazine features an invaluable index that categorizes all the recipes along dietetic lines, often adding on-the-spot bonus recipes if those in the main text don't cover all the usual courses. And to take a break from cooking, *Food & Wine* also highlights restaurants across the country and has fascinating columns on what's new in gadgets and food emporiums. For subscription information, write to *Food & Wine* magazine, 1120 Avenue of the Americas, New York, New York 10036

TIP #114 For cooking course fanatics—you don't have to give up your lessons, merely modify your curriculum.

An excellent cooking course for the dieter is one in Japanese sushi instruction. Sushi is based on the simple preparation of rice and seafood (cooked shellfish, such as crab and shrimp, raw varieties of fillet fish) and the artful slicing of Oriental vegetables. This minimal-cooking cuisine is as delicious as it is low-calorie, a tasty must for every dieter whether you learn to do it at home or enjoy it at a Japanese restaurant.

TIP #115 Start a recipe-exchange club with your dieting friends.

The more innovative and novel your recipes, the easier it'll be to stay on your diet. Make up with friends that once a week you will each be responsible for one recipe that you can write out and photocopy. For added incentive, you can all judge for a "best recipe of the month" award to go to the creator of the dish you all liked best.

Collect 7-day menu plans from your favorite women's magazines.

TIP #116

Periodicals such as *Harper's Bazaar* feature a diet a month, with 7 whole days of meals already planned for you. You can easily adapt the menus to the diet you're on (simply replace those few foods that might be taboo for you) and save yourself the drudgery of planning for a full week.

 Entertain without going off your diet, by serving buffet style.

TIP #117

A buffet allows you to present numerous dishes without your having to sample them as you would a course-by-course sit-down meal. No one will notice how little you are eating. A buffet also allows you to prepare most items in advance, freeing you from the kitchen and the course-by-course clearing of the table, too.

TIP #118

Keep your social life and your diet intact by being brave enough to serve low-cal recipes to company.

Chances are most of your guests will be watching their weight, too, and with creative cookery, the rest will never know your menu is dietetic. This poached pear recipe shows off this delicious fruit and is a great alternative to a high-cal tart.

FESTIVE TWO-COLORED POACHED PEARS

Ingredients: 4 firm ripe pears, such as Boscs,
           about 4 oz each
       white grape juice
       regular (purple) grape juice
       1 lemon, juiced
       1 stick of cinnamon, broken in 2
       4 cloves
       2 sprigs of mint

Peel, halve, and core the pears and place them in a bowl of water to which the lemon juice has been added (this prevents discoloration). In 2 separate saucepans, bring the white grape juice and the regular grape juice to a boil. Divide the pears, the cinnamon, and the cloves equally between the 2 pots. If needed, add more juice to cover the pears. Cover and reduce heat to a simmer. Let the pears cook for 10 minutes or until a knife easily pierces the fruit. Remove the pears from their poaching liquid with a slotted spoon; discard the liquid. Let the pears cool, then halve each of the pieces again. To serve, assemble the pieces into pear halves, using a quarter of each color pear (those poached in the dark juice will be a pretty rose); place 2 "halves" on each plate and garnish with mint.
Makes 4 servings; calorie count = 80.

Stick to your diet while entertaining by preparing dishes you don't happen to like!

You won't want to sample during food preparation, nor will you be tempted to overeat during the meal!

 When entertaining for the holidays, have two menus—theirs and yours.

On these special occasions, it is near impossible not to prepare certain calorie-rich traditional dishes, such as plum pudding and hard sauce or chestnut stuffing, at least for your guests. Balance the sacrifice of your not indulging in these by preparing low-cal dishes made with just you in mind. Of course, you won't be able to keep others from sampling the low-cal courses (one dieter's no-sugar, extra-tart cranberry puree was the hit of his dinner last Thanksgiving!), but you get first dibs.

 To make up for being on a calorie "budget," pay special attention to atmosphere.

The way the table is set, the way your home looks with careful lighting, with flowers arranged attractively, with an inviting fragrance in the air—these more than make up for a lack of high-calorie dishes. Bring atmosphere to your dinner table with these specifics:

- Instead of one large vase of flowers, scatter assorted bud vases on your serving table, each one holding a single unusual bloom.
- Serve a "bouquet" of raw vegetables in a wicker basket and use a hollowed head of cabbage as a holder for dip—a terrific centerpiece.
- Offer 6-inch long wooden skewers instead of the average-size toothpick for elegantly spearing single morsels of food.
- Purposely mismatch serving dishes to add a continental flavor to your table, but do use plain white or clear glass dinner plates for overall harmony.

CHAPTER 5

Eating Out

HOW TO STAY FAITHFUL ON A VARIETY OF OCCASIONS

Restaurant eating is the dieter's catch-22—you want (and need) a break from home meal planning but face temptation every time you read a menu! The following tips solve this dilemma by teaching you how to control your intake, from how to choose the right restaurant to placing a dietetic order to filling your plate at a buffet, at a party, on vacation, even at a cafeteria. Some of the ideas are unconventional, but that's what it takes to master eating out.

Eat out safely by picking a low-cal cuisine.

TIP
#122

THE TOP FIVE CHOICES
1. **Seafood**: Have fish and shellfish broiled, steamed, or poached, not fried or sauced.
2. **Japanese**: Sushi, sashimi, and soy-basted teriyaki are good choices, not batter-fried tempura.
3. **Chinese**: Ask that the chef use a minimum of peanut oil on stir-fried dishes; try steamed dishes, too.
4. **Vegetarian**: Unusual salads and vegetable dishes are delicious.
5. **Scandinavian**: Order with an emphasis on fish and lean meats.

THE FIVE WORST CHOICES

1. **French**: Calorie-laden butter sauces spell disaster.
2. **Italian**: Butter, cheese, and olive oil add up to overweight.
3. **Mexican**: Sour cream and guacamole toppings with beans undo the value of tacos and tamales.
4. **American Southern cooking**: Flour- and oil-based sauces add calories.
5. **Hungarian, Eastern European cuisines**: Too many butter- and cream-based dishes mean heavy meals...and a heavy you!

Organize a menu file.

TIP #123 Call your favorite restaurants as well as new ones you are planning to visit and request a menu by mail. Once you receive it, go over it at your leisure (on a full stomach, to avoid temptation!) and check off sensible food choices. Deciding on what to order in advance is great for those whose appetite is awakened by reading a menu—you won't even have to open it at the restaurant.

TIP #124 **If you belong to a diet center, ask your counselor to check off menu possibilities for you.**

To keep within the diet guidelines set by your group, bring the menus from your favorite restaurants with you to your next session and go over the choices with your nutritionist.

TIP #125 **Make one of your neighborhood restaurants "your" place.**

Introduce yourself to the owner, the maître d', the staff. As you become more well known, your diet needs will be met much more readily; you'll be able to have dishes cooked to your taste without any fuss or any mention of your diet in front of other guests at your table.

TIP #126 **When going to an unfamiliar restaurant, call ahead to ask if the food is prepared "to order."**

You'd be surprised at how many restaurants have most dishes premade or at least partly cooked and left to rest under a heat lamp until requested. This is not only unappetizing but also means that any specifications you might have won't be met.

 TIP #127 **When eating out, leave your credit cards behind.**

Carry only a limited amount of cash with you—knowing that you don't have your usual plastic funds will keep you from the temptation of overpriced and overrich dishes (often one and the same). Note: Use this "leave home without it" system if you are also a fan of department-store gourmet shops that honor credit cards.

TIP #128

For a low-cal food adventure, sample meatless variations of your favorite dishes.

Health food restaurants might not be as chic as others, but they offer the most alternatives for the serious dieter. Finding a low-cal dish is easy, since most are meatless and emphasize fresh produce cooked with a minimum of fuss. Items to try: soybean burgers; eggplant lasagna; pita pizza served with a sprinkling of vegetables—a delicious alternative to pepperoni.

TIP #129

Dine at restaurants that feature "à la carte" menus.

"All you can eat" and "price-fixed" menus sound like good values, but they are poor choices caloriewise, encouraging overeating. When you are presented with 5 or 6 courses at one price, it is hard to say no. Ordering à la carte gives you more choices from each course and the ability to choose from soup or an appetizer or salad instead of all 3; you'll be surprised to find yourself with a smaller check, too.

Beware of salad bars—they are potentially high-calorie.

These have sprung up at restaurants, fast-food chains, even the supermarket, making them very accessible to dieters. But unless you are very careful, the salad you make could pack a wallop! Lettuce, green veggies, and tomatoes are low-cal, but look at this chart of the more popular ingredients:

> chick-peas..........230 calories a cup!
> bacon bits..........200 calories a ½ cup!
> croutons ....125 calories an ounce!
> corn kernels........170 calories a cup!
> dressings...........125 calories a spoonful!

Also to consider: Half the nutrients of the vegetables are lost within an hour of their being sliced. Belly up to this bar with caution!

 "Ruin" your appetite before going to a restaurant.

About 30 to 60 minutes before your dinner reservation, purposely cut your appetite with a 150-calorie snack or mini-meal to put a dent in your hunger. You will find that you will order less at the restaurant, have the control to wait for the entrée to arrive, and eat less of it once it does.

TIP #132 **Place your (low-cal) drink order as soon as you are seated.**

This accomplishes two objectives: You have something to sip, and you can concentrate on your soda instead of the relish dish. Also, the drink—preferably club soda—will cut your appetite.

 TIP #133 **Ask that all high-calorie foods be removed from your table.**

Butter, nuts, oily dressings, the sugar dish—if they aren't available, you can't be tempted. Why subject yourself to them if you don't have to?

 TIP #134 **Be unconventional in your ordering.**

Example: At dinner, splurge while you keep evening eating light by ordering a double shrimp cocktail as your main course. A dozen jumbos have under 300 calories and will provoke oohs and ahhs from even die-hard filet mignon eaters. By being adventuresome, you won't feel as though you are on a diet.

Order 2 appetizers—and call it lunch!

TIP #135

Ask that one be served as the first course, the other as your entrée—but specify that you want the appetizer-sized portion of both. This method enables you to sample small servings of 2 distinct dishes and to stretch out the pleasure of your meal. Another bonus comes with your check: You save money as well as calories!

 When eating out with friends, be the first to place your order.

TIP #136

Also, refrain from asking about their choices before making yours. If not, you could be tempted into having something that sounds delicious and *is* high-calorie.

TIP #137 — When you place your order, include a side dish of lemon wedges.

A squeeze of lemon perks up all the dishes that usually come with a high-cal dressing or sauce. Use the lemon wedges throughout your meal; here are just a few of the foods it enhances:

- **Club soda:** A squeeze gives it lemon-soda taste.
- **Salad:** Combined with fresh pepper, it replaces dressing.
- **Fish:** Use instead of cocktail sauce or hollandaise.
- **Vegetables:** A sprinkling replaces a pat of butter— different but delicious just the same.

TIP #138 — When giving specifics of what to leave off your dish, ask that the chef not double up on acceptable servings to compensate.

Most restaurants wouldn't dream of serving and charging you for what looks like only a fraction of a meal, so you need to be clear about letting the waiter know the limited amount is really all you want. For example, when ordering a spinach salad without the bacon, ask your waiter not to put in an extra hard-boiled egg; or when you want a chef salad minus the high-cal cheeses, ask that the amounts of turkey and ham not be increased.

Order your salad dressings "on the side."

Oil-based dressings, even a seemingly harmless vinaigrette, can contain up to 100 calories a tablespoon. If a squeeze of lemon juice or a sprinkling of vinegar isn't enough for you, you must be the one to pour on the dressing—one tablespoon at the most, and to count it as the full 100 calories to be on the safe side.

 When ordering items served with a sauce or dip, ask that the condiment be placed on a separate dish.

Then you be the judge: If it's butter- or oil-based, refrain from using it.

 When restaurant portions exceed the serving size you're permitted, push the excess to one side of your plate and pepper heavily.

This tactic works equally well on unwanted dishes, as one of our dieting couples found last New Year's Eve. Their waiter ignored their requests and brought them salads heaped with dressing and mounds of au gratin potatoes instead of the string beans they asked for. But against even these odds, our dieters prevailed. They removed the top part of their salad, which held most of the dressing, peppered it, and then peppered the tempting potatoes. And then they crossed the restaurant off their list!

When eating out, order "half-portions" to control your intake.

TIP #142

Entrées, desserts, even appetizers can be requested in half-servings. If the restaurant isn't willing to charge you accordingly, agree to pay the regular price—you would have anyway, so count your savings in calories instead of dollars. Note: If you and a dieting friend like the same dishes, you can share single orders and split a check only half the usual size!

 ## Whenever possible, order seafood as your entrée.

TIP #143

Experiment with various cooking methods and fish varieties. Poached salmon or trout is delicious served hot or cold. Steamed mussels in a red sauce is as low-calorie as it is inexpensive. Any seafood from lobster to red snapper can be broiled "dry"—without the addition of any oil or butter.

 ## Never be intimidated into going off your diet.

TIP #144

Be confident enough to make special requests in a patient and polite way. If your waiter won't accommodate you, ask to speak to the maître d'. If you still can't get what you want, stand up and leave!

Always eat the parsley.

A sprig of parsley has one calorie, terrific amounts of vitamins A and C, and a variety of minerals, including potassium, calcium, and iron—all very much needed by the dieter. Plus it leaves a refreshing taste in your mouth!

 Ask that the check be brought with your entrée.

Having the completed bill in front of you will help you resist the temptation of ordering dessert.

 Before ordering fresh fruit at a restaurant, ask if it has been sweetened with sugar syrup.

Many restaurants add this high-cal flavor enhancer automatically when making fruit salad or serving berries; as the syrup is clear, it is almost indiscernible—the only way to know for sure is to ask your waiter to ask the restaurant's pastry/dessert chef. If it has been added, skip dessert, or buy your own fruit on your way home, to avoid seeing a surprise on your scale!

Try to limit restaurant eating to one meal a day.

Because every low-calorie meal you order in a restaurant is essentially a sacrifice—who wouldn't rather have an elaborate and high-cal meal prepared for them?—too many meals out can add up to temptation. If your business necessitates meetings at mealtime, arrange a working lunch or dinner (or breakfast) at your desk with attractive salads or lean-meat sandwiches (with mustard, not mayo!).

TIP #149

Play with your food!

Especially when you're on a date with a new interest or out with a business acquaintance and don't want to bring up the subject of your diet, it's the best way to pretend you're eating up a storm when you don't want to. Cut your food into pieces, move it all over your plate—just don't raise your fork to your mouth once you've eaten the quantity you're allowed. And if your partner catches on, simply explain you're too interested in him or her and the conversation to eat.

TIP #150

When you are looking for a fast club-soda pick-me-up, try a fast-food restaurant.

Most have a soda dispenser that mixes flavored syrups with carbonated water along a row of pumps; one of these delivers soda without the mix. You might have to explain this to the counter attendant, but your effort will be rewarded.

TIP #151

Resist buying food from street vendors.

This type of food-on-the-run eating is not at all satisfying and usually high-calorie. Ice cream bars (calorie count = 250), soft pretzels (calorie count = 350), and frankfurters (calorie count = 300)—the typical vendor fare—aren't smart food choices when you're on a limited budget and tend to be forgotten soon after consumed. Note: If you have no choice or if you find yourself sneaking a bite of your friend's hot dog, add the entry to your journal immediately (see tip #9). Calorie count of a good-sized hot dog bite = 50.

When you are invited to a dinner party, phone ahead to ask about the menu.

TIP #152

Of course, this is tactful only when the dinner is being given by a friend who knows you are on a diet. The purpose is to give you the opportunity to review what you will or won't be able to eat and to rough out a calorie count for your journal (see tip #9). Writing in your portions in advance will lessen the temptation to pick at additional foods once at the party.

 When you are invited to a dinner party whose menu offers no low-calorie choices, offer to bring a dish of your own making.

TIP #153

Suggest a recipe that will harmonize with your host or hostess's other courses and present it in a clear glass receptacle that won't conflict with other serving pieces. The following carrot salad is a good choice—pretty and not obviously dietetic.

CARROT SALAD VINAIGRETTE

Ingredients:
    2 lbs carrots, peeled and grated
    2 red peppers, seeded and grated
    4 tbsps raisins
    4 tbsps of safflower oil
    6 tbsps of balsamic vinegar
    1 tbsp of dijon-style mustard

Toss the carrots with the peppers and raisins. In a small dish, whisk the vinegar and the dijon, then blend in the oil, drop by drop. Add 2 tablespoons of water as you continue to whisk. Pour the dressing over the carrot mixture and toss to dress thoroughly. Marinate in the fridge for 2 hours, stirring up the dressing every 30 minutes.

Makes 8 servings; calorie count per serving = 105.

If after calling ahead you learn that the menu at a formal dinner is prohibited on your diet, decline the invitation.

TIP #154

An extreme measure, true, but the only way to avoid backtracking. One of our dieters was invited to an Italian smorgasbord feast of great caloric proportions. In his case, the situation was complicated by the fact that the dinner was in honor of a special friend. He decided to explain his dilemma to the friend; she understood and accepted his refusal without unfair pressure. The two made a raincheck date to make up for it: She had a second celebration that allowed him to stay on his diet!

When you want to splurge at an upcoming party, plan for it with a diet "vacation."

TIP #155

You can give yourself one evening off, but "save" for it by cutting back 100 calories each of the 5 preceding days and again, afterward, for the next 3. On the day of the party, eat lightly, but don't starve yourself. And chances are you won't go too far off in the space of a few hours. Make another deal with yourself: Don't get on the scale first thing the next morning—you might experience a slight and temporary water weight gain from the extra liquids in your system. Seeing this could set you back psychologically and for no reason at all. Just resume your diet as suggested above, feeling good that you can get yourself back on track, the real challenge.

On all social occasions, pour your own wine.

Two ounces is an acceptable serving. If your host or hostess insists on refilling your glass, let it "breathe" all evening. If your host or hostess tries to badger you into drinking more, explain that tomorrow is your first volunteer session at the local office of MADD (Mothers Against Drunk Driving). Be outspoken if you must—remember, no one can lose the weight for you.

 At a party, always have a glass of club soda (or seltzer) in your hand.

This keeps well-meaning revelers from thrusting ones filled with high-calorie liquor in your direction.

 At a holiday dinner, plan your meal around one special food you have been craving all year.

Decide up front whether it's stuffing or potatoes! You may have small tastes of up to four other dishes. That's all! Remember: There are always leftovers for tomorrow.

 At a holiday party, never drink eggnog.

The cholesterol-laden ingredients will ruin you and your diet. Enjoy this hot mulled cider instead.

HOT HOLIDAY CIDER

Ingredients: 8 oz apple cider
1 stick cinnamon
2 cloves
dash of allspice

Place all the ingredients in a saucepan and heat just
to the boiling point. Strain into a mug.
Makes one serving; calorie count = 100.

 **Learn how to navigate a buffet
TIP
#160** **table.**

When faced with this kind of choice, the average dieter
crumbles. But our savvy dieters have devised a strategy
that spells satisfaction without straying from your weight-
loss plan. Follow these steps as outlined:

1. Satisfy your eyes by taking a slow, comprehensive tour of the table. Take a few minutes to
   absorb what you saw and to draw up a plan of
   action.
2. Fill two-thirds of your plate with vegetables, raw
   or cooked.
3. When you come upon a dish you absolutely must
   try, use the single-bite approach (see tip #49).
   Limit yourself to 3 choices.
4. Gravitate toward lean meats sliced to order (by
   now you know what 4 ounces looks like—see
   tip #88 to refresh your memory).
5. Stay away from anything creamed or not readily
   identifiable: too many unknown calories.

TIP #161

Avoid happy hour bars that offer free hors d'oeuvres.

These are usually the greasy, hard-to-resist type of appetizer—and how many times have you said no to food that was free?

TIP #162

Limit the number of drink dates in your social calendar.

Make yourself a promise each time you schedule such a date: You will stop with one drink and have club soda for the rest of the evening. If you cannot keep this promise, try meeting in a public atrium rather than a bar.

TIP #163

Brown-bag it with style!

Eating at your desk is a viable alternative to coping with a restaurant lunch on a daily basis. Jazz up your brown-bag meal with a linen napkin and a pretty china plate that you can rinse and store in your desk. Buy a few assorted plastic containers so that you aren't limited to sandwiches and fill them with low-cal goodies. Here are three ideas:

1. alfalfa sprouts, cherry tomatoes, raisins, and cashew nuts;
2. crabmeat and cole slaw;
3. cold pasta in diet dressing with herbs and sunflower seeds.

When working at your desk through lunch, keep your meal order simple.

When deadlines catch you unprepared and force you to order in, select a plain salad and 2 juices. You won't be able to give your food the concentration you ought to, so don't treat yourself to a special dish. Do make up for this hasty meal by taking a midafternoon break and having a light snack, such as frozen yogurt. Have it out of your office if possible, to clear your mind, or at least away from your desk.

 ### Turn your morning business meeting into a jogging breakfast.

The new trend of mixing breakfast with a meeting can easily ruin your day, caloriewise, by 9:30 A.M.! Many weight-conscious executives have devised a better plan— rather than eat and talk, they jog and do business! After a healthy mile (or more) run, toast with a refreshing glass of grapefruit juice to seal your deal!

 ### At a business lunch, order the simplest food available.

Tried-and-true staples, such as chef's salad or cottage cheese and half a melon, are perfect choices. Avoid food that will distract you from the matters at hand; this is no time for the fun display of tableside Caesar salad preparation. (Save that for an unconventional *dinner entrée* when you're among friends.)

TIP #167

At a business dinner, indulge in a roll or slice of bread (without butter) as soon as the bread basket is served.

Surprised? Well, in addition to its being an excellent food source (see tip #17), having it at the start of your dinner will satisfy you; cut the hunger that can easily drive you crazy as you wait for the first course to arrive; and keep you from developing "starving eyes" (a dieting side effect) that garner unwanted attention (like being asked, "Are you on a diet?"—information you probably won't want to divulge to business acquaintances).

TIP #168

At the office party, be prepared with excuses for why you aren't drinking and getting sloshed like everyone else.

These keep you from having to tell one and all about your no-liquor diet. Try the following "white lies."

- "I'm taking head cold medication."
- "I'm having dinner with the in-laws later—have to keep my wits about me!"
- "The big boss asked to see me in his office."

If you are dieting at college, buy your meals as you go.

Avoid enrolling in a prepaid (and expensive) meal plan that gives you access to unlimited portions of food. This is how thin students gain college overweight: Stress sends them to the commissary, the next best thing to their home kitchen! If, on the other hand, you are on a strict budget, you'll be conservative in your food selections. Note: If you are in high school, use this same pay-as-you-go system at the cafeteria or bring your own lunch for a stricter calorie watch.

 On campus, use the student lounge, not the commissary, as a meeting place.

The less you are around food, the less tempted you'll be to eat.

 When vacationing, try to choose from a restaurant's list of daily specials.

These dishes are determined by that day's market availability and are sure to be among the freshest items on the menu. And fresh means less need for other ingredients that add calories, making the special of the day the low-cal choice...without sacrificing taste.

TIP #172 **Plan ahead when vacationing with a relative or a friend: Let your diet needs be known.**

Call in advance to explain that no elaborate cooking is necessary for your visit and bring whatever staples you can with you. Once there, offer to pay for any special items you'll need. A little forethought means a vacation without food anxiety and with weight loss.

 TIP #173 **When traveling to a foreign country, be prepared with a list of key phrases to explain your dietary needs.**

The Special Diet Foreign Phrase Book, by Helen Saltz Jacobson (Rodale Press, 1963), is an excellent volume. Your culinary vocabulary should include:

- "Please bring the sauce on the side."
- "Please bring me mineral water."
- "Please cook my food without oil or butter."
- "Do you have any fresh fish? Fresh fruit?"

 TIP #174 **When traveling, investigate each region's low-calorie food specialties.**

Whether you plan your vacation according to which country's food you like best or are the kind of traveler who can find a satisfying meal anywhere, you should know that no matter where you travel, you can eat well and not gain weight. Use this basic planner as a guide:

96

COUNTRY	FOODS TO TRY	FOODS TO AVOID
Mexico	grilled meats; seafood; chicken tacos, in moderation	bean and rice dishes; cornmeal-based dishes
the Caribbean	native seafood; tropical fruits	coconut drinks; starch-based dishes
Canada	salmon, grilled and smoked	same as home
the Orient	roasted pork and other marinated and grilled meats; lightly stir-fried dishes; seafood, raw or cooked	breaded and deep-fried dishes; dumplings and wontons
France and the Benelux countries	poultry and beef dishes with wine sauces; fruit sorbets	dishes in cream, butter, or cheese sauces; cream pastries
Italy	chicken, veal, or pasta in tomato sauces; vegetables lightly sautéed in olive oil	pasta in heavy cream, butter or cheese sauces; cannoli and other pastries
Spain	grilled meats; seafood dishes such as paella	rich sauces
Germany	lean smoked meats; vegetable salads	dumplings, heavy potato dishes; Bavarian pastries
England	roasts, lean and sliced to order	meat pies with heavy pastry crusts
Middle East	lamb; eggplant	too much rice and kasha; phyllo-dough pastries

On vacation, make lunch your big meal of the day.

You can burn off most calories during afternoon sight-seeing activities. If you are in a country where dinner is served quite late, such as Brazil, eat sparingly or not at all: Not every local custom has to be observed, only those that fit your diet.

 When traveling in Europe, put together your own meals from gourmet food shops.

These provide a great alternative to constant restaurant eating, offering quality foods with portions you control. Use this equivalency chart to gauge your serving sizes:

100 grams = 3.5 oz
¼ kilo = 18 oz
½ kilo = 1 lb

Note: When you want to apply the one-bite system to sample a food (see tip #49), ask for 25 or 50 grams.

 Be prepared with a mini-meal when going on long day trips at home or on vacation.

A can of juice, a 1-ounce piece of cheese, and a whole fruit, such as an apple or a peach, will satisfy you if you can't find an acceptable restaurant in your travels. What you can almost always find is a small roll or individual loaf of bread to round out your meal—one of the safest foods you can eat anywhere in the world.

If you want to take a cruise, make it a "floating spa" vacation.

TIP #178

The average cruise is an open invitation to indulge—6 scheduled meals and unscheduled food on demand add up to extra pounds. However, floating spa cruises, specially designed for weight loss through luxurious diet and exercise plans, are a fabulous alternative when you want to be at sea. For the most pampering experience write to Cunard Line Ltd., 555 Fifth Avenue, New York, N.Y. 10017, for information about their spa cruise on the famed *QE 2.*

 When vacationing in the sun, avoid high-cal tropical drinks.

TIP #179

The sun and liquor don't mix any better than dieting and drinking do—Caribbean concoctions, for instance, can be lethal! If you have alcohol allowances on your regimen, satisfy them with wine, preferably in the evening.

 Eliminate all diet dairy products from your diet when traveling outside of the United States.

TIP #180

Few countries process their milk as we do (even certain cheeses made abroad and shipped to this country are made differently from the same brands sold in their place of origin); the American body is not always able to digest it. The thrill of indulging in unhomogenized milk, with its thick cream floating on top of the bottle, can leave you very ill, all the wonderful eighteenth-century English literature aside. And unfortunately, even low-cal variations can, too.

Avoid mixing business with the pleasure of nonstop expense-account eating when you must travel for your job.

Eat as though you were at home or, better yet, as though you were paying for everything you ate!

CHAPTER 6

Exercise Sense

HOW TO BEGIN AND EXPAND A FITNESS PROGRAM

Dieting means exercise——→there's no getting around it, but it can be fun. Exercise defines your figure, determines good health, burns calories, and speeds weight loss. But start gradually to avoid the over-do——→fast burnout——→give-up cycle that hits many an overzealous dieter. Easy does it. This section comes with the stamp of approval of fitness consultant and author Dr. Michael D. Wolf, whose research documents the very direct relationship between exercise and the body you want to have. *You should consult your physician before beginning any exercise program.*

Walk, every chance you get!

TIP
#182

Walking burns off calories, and that leads to weight loss. Use it as the first step in your get-active plan: Start by walking everywhere you usually drive to. Begin at a slow pace, then, as you become more accustomed to walking, work at quickening your step. Use every opportunity: Walk to work, to the market, up and down stairs, back and forth when you're on the telephone; all these little expenditures add up to lost pounds!

Before starting a comprehensive fitness regimen, have a fitness evaluation at a sports-training institute.

TIP #183

A workout pro can both design a program that meets your body reshaping needs and motivate you to reach your goals. This kind of coaching is invaluable, especially if you plan on exercising at home. Periodic reevaluations will enable you to rechannel your efforts as needed and give you the impetus to strive for new endurance levels.

 When beginning or increasing your exercise program, work slowly and gradually.

TIP #184

If, for example, you are starting a workout on a stationary bike, limit your first session to 5 minutes, then add on slowly. If you aimed for 20 right off the bat, all you would achieve would be soreness, fatigue, and a great desire to abandon the program before it even got under way. Like portion control, this aspect of dieting is something you develop a little at a time. Enthusiasm is terrific, but don't use it up all at once.

 Be properly equipped for the fitness activities you've chosen.

TIP #185

For almost every exercise, this means starting with the correct footwear, including socks. For women, a sports bra is recommended regardless of your bra size. If you are engaging in rigorous activity, such as roller-skating, elbow and knee pads are in order. Consider an ankle support if this is a weak area; sweatbands if you perspire heavily; leg warmers if you have poor circulation. Fancy sweats or a jogging outfit isn't a must but can brighten your mood.

TIP #186 Always stretch before exercise and always warm up before stretching.

Warm-ups and stretches are different activities. Warm-ups stimulate muscles; stretching makes them limber and flexible. Contrary to the advice given in most exercise programs, muscles must be warmed up before they can be stretched. Think of taffy: It needs to be warmed before it can be pulled; if not, it would break off. To warm up, try an easy 5-minute walk or a slow-speed pedal on a stationary bike.

 ### TIP #187 Use yoga to get your body into condition for high-cal burning forms of exercise.

Yoga is a series of postures that increases your flexibility, making you more limber and more agile, making it easier for you to add on more strenuous activity. Yoga is a great way to start your day; the only caution is to avoid straining in any one of its positions—go into a stretch only as far as feels comfortable. Get yourself started with a book that covers the basics or with one of the many TV fitness programs for a more personal "demonstration": "Stretch with Priscilla" and "Lilias, Yoga and You" are two good choices.

 ### TIP #188 To progress to a moderate activity, try calisthenics.

Doing 10 repetitions of an exercise, such as this tummy tightener, during each commercial of a 30-minute TV show is a great way to get into the habit. You'll feel a few twinges at first, but remember that your being out of shape is what hurts you, not the exercise itself!

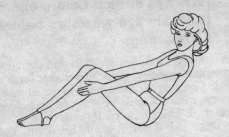

1. Start with feet flat on the floor, arms straight in front of you.

2. Raise your feet to straighten your legs and swing arms out to the sides for balance. Hold for three seconds.

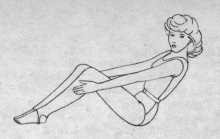

3. At the same time, bring arms and feet back to the starting position.

4. Repeat throughout each commercial. Do 9 or as many more as you can.

 TIP #189 **To increase the difficulty of calisthenic exercises and burn off extra calories, use wrist and ankle weights.**

These cuffs wrap around you and are secured with Velcro closures. Start with 1-pound weights and progress to cuffs of 5 pounds each, in ½- to 1-pound increments. (You can wear these whenever convenient during the day.)

TIP #190 **Whittle your waist with sit-ups.**

This variation of the usual chin-to-knee exercise is tough but brings results. (It also makes a great appetite suppressant!)

1. Lie flat on the floor with your body perpendicular to your bed.

2. Bring your knees into your chest and wriggle your body toward the bed until your buttocks are flush with the side of the bed. Then swing your calves onto the mattress. Your body should form a Z shape.
3. Cross your arms over your chest and tuck your chin into your neck. Take a deep breath.
4. Breathe out and lift your head, shoulders, and upper back off the floor toward your knees.
5. Breathe in as you roll down to the floor.
6. Aim for 10 to 15 repetitions. Gradually work up to 25.

 TIP #191 **Try weight lifting to dramatically change the shape of your body.**

Working out with weights creates muscle, which has 2 diet-boosting advantages. First, the body uses up more calories to sustain muscle than fat. Second, muscle improves the look of your body by giving you attractive, firm, and sexy definition. Women should note that without ample amounts of testosterone, the "male hormone," they need not worry about developing unsightly bulges. To discover more about weights, visit a Nautilus training center (see the *Yellow Pages* of your phone book) or buy Dr. Michael D. Wolf's excellent paperback *The Complete Book of Nautilus Training* (Contemporary Books, 1984).

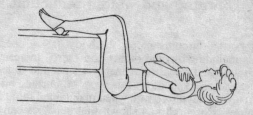

1. Swing your calves onto the bed or chair; cross your arms and inhale.

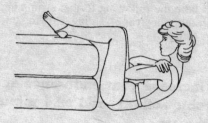

2. Exhale and curl your head and shoulders toward your knees.

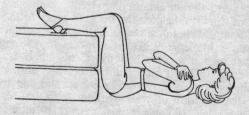

3. Inhale as you relax to the floor; repeat immediately.

Discover aerobics for high-cal burning and weight reduction.

TIP #192

Under normal circumstances, the body uses a chemical process including oxygen (hence the "aero" in aerobics) to burn food and release the energy we need to function. Aerobic exercise speeds up this process, burning off calories at a very advanced rate when maintained for at least 10 minutes. Research has shown that aerobics can also slow the aging process, improve heart function, and create a strong power base of endurance and stamina. It is the most efficient exercise system for burning the most calories and can take the following forms: swimming, running, cycling, jumping rope, skiing, rowing, aerobic dancing. Start today!

 To increase your endurance at aerobic activity, add on 1 minute each day.

TIP #193

As noted in tip #192, 10 minutes of aerobic activity can constitute a workout. But to burn off the fat that is stored in the body (those unsightly bulges!), you need to boost your workouts to a minimum of 30 minutes, roughly the amount of time it takes for the body to produce the enzymes (a natural chemical reaction) that seek out fat and break it down into energy. As added incentive, you should know that regular aerobic activity of this length boosts your overall ability to burn calories not just during exercise but for hours afterward. The easiest and safest way to raise the duration of your workout is to add to it 1 minute each day. If you are now cycling 10 minutes a day, for example, in a week you'll be up to 17; in 2 weeks, 24 minutes. Have as your ultimate goal 60 minutes at least 3 times a week: The results will be more than worth your effort.

TIP #194 **Create your own gym at home.**

All you need is a corner of your bedroom or den. Start with an exercise mat or, if your floor is carpeted, a brightly colored mover's pad for extra cushioning. That's all you need to begin a calisthenics/and a yoga program. When you're ready to increase your workout, consider these options:

- **for aerobics**: a stationary bike or a treadmill for running, or a rowing or skiing machine, or a high-quality jump rope;
- **for weight lifting**: an all-in-one machine, such as West Bend's Total Gym, that offers more than 70 exercises in one unit or, if you prefer free weights, a set of dumbbells with weight rings to increase poundage, and a bench press.

TIP #195 **To get the most weight loss benefits from your exercise sessions, schedule each activity at the appropriate time of day.**

Yoga is best suited for the morning: Its actions remove early-morning kinks and energize you for the day ahead. Calisthenics can be performed whenever they are most convenient for you. Aerobics should be undertaken just before dinner: The energy level required raises your metabolism, helping you burn more calories at night (at a time the body is usually winding down), and helps diminish evening appetite. A weight workout could be scheduled as late as possible, because its anaerobic (non-oxygen-producing) action tires you—great for getting a good night's sleep.

To protect yourself, carefully control your exercise climate.

The ideal temperature is in the low-70-degree range, but a more vital statistic is the humidity factor—over 50% and you could be in a danger zone, even when the temperature is low. On a hot and muggy day, use air-conditioning to remove extra humidity indoors and avoid exercising outdoors altogether. In cold weather, protect yourself at the start of exercise by layering your clothes; as your body heats up, individual layers can be peeled off.

 Set up a weekly exercise schedule.

Fix the time and the days of the week for the variety of activities you practice, then record them in your datebook. Then try to schedule social activities around them. (If you start letting other dates take precedence, your good intentions will be for nothing.) Here is a sample itinerary for the experienced fitness buff:

Aerobics: Monday, Wednesday, Friday; time: 5:30–6:15 P.M.
Weight work: Tuesday, Saturday; 8–9 P.M.
Brisk walk or sport activity: Sunday; 11–12 noon.

TIP #198

Keep a progress record to further motivate yourself.

Note every strength increase, every minute spent exercising, every pound lifted, every rep accomplished. Review your progress weekly to remind yourself of all the fitness strides you've made and to encourage you to set higher fitness goals for the coming weeks. Note: Rather than have a second notebook, you might make this part of your diet journal (see tip #9).

TIP #199

Exercise with your family.

To spend extra time with your kids as you burn off those calories, plan a family exercise outing every Sunday afternoon—everyone has fun. During the week, encourage other parent-child workouts: a 20-minute exercise period before dinner; a mother-daughter dance class; a father-son basketball game in the yard; and vice versa (boys can benefit from the flexibility taught in dance; girls need the aerobic training of the ball game).

TIP #200

Tailor your fitness program to the seasons.

Variety helps you sustain interest. And by taking advantage of what each time of year has to offer, you can enjoy being outdoors as you burn off calories. In summer, swim twice a week. In the fall, put on your hiking boots and visit nearby parks. In the winter, retrieve your old ice skates or skis. In the spring, take the bike out of the garage and pedal yourself into shape.

· ·
TIP
#201

Always have a contingency plan when scheduling outdoor activities.

(See tip #201). This way, if it should rain on the day of your cross-country trek, you won't give yourself an excuse to miss exercising. Here are three great indoor alternatives:

1. TV exercise programs on cable or home video exercise cassettes for use on your VCR;
2. a mini-rebounder for indoor trampoline-style jumping and running; use it without sneakers, with fast-beat music for impetus;
3. do 100 leg lifts (each side), holding for 5 seconds in the up phase of each rep.

· ·
TIP
#202

Exercise with a partner.

Ask a fitness-minded friend to work out with you. If you both set important fitness goals and support each other's effort, you'll increase your chance of success. If you know that another person depends on you to show up for a cal class or a run around the lake, you'll be much more likely to stick to your plan. And you'll provide the same incentive for your partner. Note: Don't let age discourage you—one group of post-60 ladies I know meets 3 times a week at their local high school and speed-walks around the track for 45 minutes!

Drink plenty of water throughout exercise to keep your body well hydrated.

TIP #203

Have a glassful 15 to 30 minutes before exercise and keep 1 handy to sip from during your workout, especially an aerobic one. Don't chug down too much, too fast—the body can only handle about 6 oz every 15 minutes, but sipping is fine and necessary to replenish body fluids lost through perspiration.

 Drink up after exercise to combat hunger pangs.

TIP #204

Exercise does cut your appetite once you get into a serious regimen. However, during the first week or 2, it might leave you hungry. Follow up your workout with 2 glasses of water both to continue the rehydration process described in the previous tip and to put a check on your hunger. Then slowly sip 4 ounces of fruit juice or 6 ounces of vegetable juice to satisfy your urge.

 Counter fatigue with extra sleep, not extra portions.

TIP #205

A boost in your quota of exercise coupled with your reduced calorie intake can drain you of some of your energy at first. Compensate by getting a minimum of 8 hours' sleep every night, even if this means curtailing your social life a bit. If you start feeling run-down, you might be tempted to give up exercise, and that would be a mistake.

TIP #206

Exercise can become its own reward.

After putting yourself through a rigorous training session, such as an aerobic workout, you'll be in better shape to get physical in a fun way: roller-skating to dance music or touring the countryside on your 10-speed. Both these forms of "whole body" exercise will burn up calories—and they don't feel like work! The key is your attitude: Never look on fitness as a drudgery; think of it as energizing!

TIP #207

Be careful not to expend great effort on low-calorie burning forms of exercise.

If the activity isn't aerobic or muscle building, consider it as leisure, not a workout. Many people mistakenly think that their three rounds of bowling and their beachside volleyball game are exercise equivalents; they aren't. Although more calories are burned than if you spent that time sleeping, the difference is far from great. Example: Sleeping burns 60 calories an hour, bowling burns 85, volleyball, 180; now compare those figures to an aerobic activity like cycling, which can use up to 600 calories an hour! Other low-calorie activities popularly mistaken for high-cal burners are badminton, archery, croquet, table tennis, and golfing (when you use a cart). You needn't give up your favorite pastimes; just be sure to count them in addition to exercise.

Avoid "effortless" exercise
TIP
#208 **gimmicks and gadgets.**

Any exercise "aid" or machine that promises to lose the weight for you is a hoax. Reducing machines do nothing more than jiggle you around. Gadgets like one widely advertised elastic weight loss belt "guaranteed" by the manufacturer to whittle off inches can't possibly remove fat. Only you can expend the energy and do the work that will melt those pounds—and that is that!

 Give up looking for excuses to
TIP
#209 **quit.**

You can exercise with a cold, even with menstrual cramps (exercise can often alleviate them!). If you don't have 30 minutes, spend 15 minutes working out. You can always do something—even sore muscles can be worked on, gently, after a warm-up, with stretches.

 When considering a health club or
TIP
#210 **gym, look for the one that meets**
your individual requirements.

Flexible hours, a frequent number of classes, and the most up-to-date equipment will keep your program varied and interesting. Also evaluate the amenities—whether they provide towels and exercise gear or lockers to store your own in (important if you commute to work and want a gym near the office), whether they offer a snack bar for post-workout meals, whether the staff is available for personal instruction, whether the atmosphere is conducive to serious exercise. Draw up a list of your needs and evaluate each possibility carefully. A gym is an important fitness investment.

TIP #211 To get the most weight loss benefits from your gym, discuss your goals with your instructor or fitness pro as soon as possible.

The staff should do more than supervise or teach classes; they should be able to evaluate your needs and design a program for you: They know which forms of exercise you need for body reshaping. In addition to your day-to-day requirements, follow up this initial meeting with periodic checks at least once a month to help you increase your performance.

TIP #212 At the gym, be sure to compete only with yourself.

Try not to make the mistake of judging yourself against others in your class or in the weight room: This will lead you to push yourself too hard or, conversely, to get discouraged and give up. Yes, motivate yourself to try harder but always at your own pace.

TIP #213 Use your health club's luxury features as incentives for giving an all-out effort.

The hot tub comes *after* a grueling exercise class. Have a massage *after* you lose 2 inches from your hips. Visit the juice bar *after* a weight workout during which you increased your resistance by 10 pounds.

**To increase your exercise output,
plan a "walking" vacation.**

TIP
#214

Visit a large city, anywhere from our country to a European capital. Walk everywhere you can—it's good exercise and by far the best way to appreciate a new place. Plan ahead using local maps to chart a daily expedition of at least 2 hours. For the most comfort, wear the best running shoes you can afford: The extra cushioning and fitted arches will keep your feet in top form throughout the length of your trip!

 **When vacationing under the sun,
make the beach your gym.**

TIP
#215

You can adapt your exercise plan to your surroundings and not miss any of the fitness strategy you left at home. Take a brisk walk on the sand to tone legs (run only if you have no ankle or knee problems—the beach is not the perfect track, as some will tell you!). Make snow angels on the sand to give your arms and legs a calisthenic treat. Take your leg lifts into the water—pool or ocean—it acts as invisible "weight cuffs" making each action more difficult as you fight its gravity. Then try 10 minutes of serious swimming or strong kicks as you hold the side of the pool or an ocean-mate as your anchor. Back home, you'll be surprised with the progress you'll have made.

TIP #216

When traveling on business, without time for the usual forms of physical fitness, go prepared with a grab bag of exercises.

To counter muscle neglect, devise your very own mix of calisthenics to do for 10 to 20 minutes daily, in the morning or at night, before bed. Leg lifts, donkey kicks, arm swings are all good—or you might even create your own exercises. As long as you do something, you'll stay in the habit and look forward to resuming your more rigorous plan as soon as you get home.

CHAPTER 7

Boosting Weight Loss

TECHNIQUES TO INCREASE RESULTS

Successful dieting necessitates change: You need to make a series of small, daily adjustments to start living thin. One of the most important is boosting your activity level. The more active you are, the faster your body metabolizes, or burns, calories and then digs into your fat stores for energy. The tips in this chapter are designed to make you more active and to energize you for increased results.

· · ·
TIP #217

To help your body consume calories most efficiently, keep each meal under 400 calories.

The human body can metabolize (or "handle") only that much energy at one time—any extra calories are automatically stored as fat. That's why you can hold your weight with 5 400-calorie meals but would gain weight if you ate 1 2000-calorie meal! Also, small meals tend to "shrink" the stomach—you feel full on less food; the more you eat large meals, the more food it takes to reach the point of fullness. To show you just how far 400 calories can be stretched, here are three examples:

1. **Breakfast**: 6 oz apple juice (75); English muffin with 1 tsp butter (160); 4 oz cherry yogurt (125); total = 360.

2. **Lunch**: 1 cup tomato-vegetable soup (80); shrimp salad of 4 oz shrimp and 1 tbsp low-cal imitation mayonnaise (200); ½ cantaloupe (40); 3 breadsticks (75); total = 395.

3. **Dinner**: salad nicoise of 3½ oz tuna (120), 4 oz string beans (30), 4 oz red potatoes (70), 4 oz cherry tomatoes (25), 5 large black olives (25) sprinkled with 1 tbsp vinegar (2) and ½ tbsp of oil (60); 4 oz tangerine (40); total = 372.

Reverse the size of your meals: Eat a big breakfast and a small dinner.

TIP #218

Your body burns calories more efficiently when you are active—it makes sense, then, to eat a larger meal at breakfast, a slightly smaller one at lunch, and a very light meal for dinner (after which you're likely to be sedentary). You'll not only lose weight faster; you'll find it much easier to sleep.

 If you work at home, resist going back to sleep after seeing off your spouse and kids.

TIP #219

Energize yourself and raise your calorie-burning metabolism by getting right into your day. If you need to, take a short nap before lunch or after midday exercise.

 Find ways to burn extra calories with a slight variation in everyday activities.

TIP #220

Here are 4 examples:

- If your home has a staircase, make as many trips as you can, climbing them 2 at a time if possible.
- Pick up your children after school on foot whenever possible (if the school is more than ½ mile from home, drive part of the way only).
- Instead of simply letting the dog out in the yard, exercise the pet yourself in a nearby park—he gets lonely playing fetch by himself!
- Make a challenge of doing your major housecleaning as swiftly as possible. Clock yourself and then break your record by moving faster the next time—consider the extra time free minutes for your own enjoyment.

TIP #221 **To help you be more active after work, turn on your favorite music when you get home at night.**

A fast tempo will reenergize you and keep you from collapsing into the nearest chair. And that, in turn, means you'll burn more calories and lose weight faster.

 TIP #222 **If you work at home, plan at least one activity that gets you out of the house every day...then try to walk to your destination.**

The activity keeps you from thinking about food and burns extra calories not just while you are doing it but as you get yourself ready to go out, too. Most important, you feel energized and good about yourself, which, in turn, increases your desire to be thin.

 TIP #223 **Make love, not lasagna.**

Lovemaking, and all the wonderful steps that lead up to it, is quite an efficient calorie burner, about 250 calories every encounter. And what better way to get your mind off food?

TIP #224 **Fill up your dance card, at least once a week.**

To get all the benefits of exercise with a lot more pleasure, make a weekly dance date with a special romantic interest or a group of unattached friends if you prefer to go solo. Slow dancing can burn up to 300 calories an hour and disco dancing up to twice that! What are you waiting for?

Cancel out extra snack calories with exercise.

TIP #225

Next time a craving leads you to the corner grocery and a bag of potato chips, make a deal with yourself on the spot: To eat 1 ounce of chips, you must first exercise to burn off the caloric equivalent in addition to any exercise you have already done or have yet to do. In Potato Chipese that translates to 150 calories or 15 minutes of strenuous cycling. Here are other trades:

- 1 oz of pretzels ....10 minutes of aerobics
- 1 chocolate chip cookie..... 10 minutes of jumping jacks
- 1 ice cream sandwich... 30 minutes of calisthenics
- 1 milk shake, extra thick ..... 45 minutes of swimming
- 1 jelly donut ....20 minutes of racquetball
- 1 slice of apple pie.......... 30 minutes of running
- 1 piece of chocolate fudge cake ..... 60 minutes of cross-country skiing!

 Plan a diet vacation at a luxurious spa.

TIP #226

Call them fat farms or reducing resorts, these first-class accommodations make you feel pampered as the pounds melt off. Each of the following spas provides continuous supervision, a full program of exercise, nutrition, and beauty counseling, as well as the tastiest of diet meals. One or 2 (expensive—$2,000 is average) weeks is a great way to launch a diet or to give you 1 last push to drop those few remaining pounds. Contact them directly for more information.

- The World of Palm-Aire—Pompano Beach, Florida, 800-327-4960.
- The Bonaventure Intercontinental Hotel and Spa—Fort Lauderdale, Florida, 800-327-8090.
- Gurney's Inn—Montauk, New York, 516-668-2345.
- The Greenhouse—Arlington, Texas, 817-640-4000.
- The Golden Door—Escondido, California, 619-744-5777.
- La Costa Resort Hotel and Spa—Carlsbad, California, 619-438-9111.

TIP #227 Try a 24-hour juice fast to cleanse your body and lose excess water weight

Fasting usually means abstaining from all food and beverages, with, perhaps, the exception of water. A juice fast is less severe—your body has a rest from solid foods but is still supplied with some nutrients. Follow these guidelines carefully:

1. Do not fast for more than 24 hours without medical supervision.
2. Drink at least 10 glasses of water on your fast day.
3. Drink 500 calories' worth of vegetable and/or fruit juices, preferably 4 oz every 1–2 hours.

You should consult your physician before fasting.

CHAPTER 8

Staying Motivated

INCENTIVES FOR DIETING

Motivation is the mental part of a diet. To stick to your plan, you need to keep yourself psyched with strong incentives—your reasons for wanting to be thin. And to combat the feelings of frustration and of depression (which dieting often brings and which can be a stronger temptation to cheat than a favorite food), you need to learn techniques for maintaining a positive frame of mind.

Motivate yourself by composing a list of all the advantages of being thin.

And put "personal satisfaction" at the very top. The desire for self-improvement is the drive needed to get you on a diet and to get you to stay on it. Review the list often—carry it with you—to maintain your dedication.

 Give yourself $5 for every week you stick with your diet.

Put it toward a luxury item you really want. Also add $2 to this "diet piggy bank" every time you lose a pound. As soon as you have saved and lost enough, buy the item on your dream list. Knowing that every week and each lost pound will bring you closer to calling that luxury your own helps keep you on your diet.

Target upcoming social events as mini-milestones for weight loss.

For example, if your sister's anniversary party is 1 month away, use it as incentive to lose your next 3 pounds. The day after the party, choose another social event to aim for; if your calendar is a bit empty, buy yourself theater tickets or plan a gathering of your own. These special motivation boosters provide terrific reinforcement to your dedication—and the months of exciting dates circled on your wall will add up to weight loss success.

 To renew your incentive, do your swimsuit shopping in January and February.

During these months, department stores feature "cruise" season selections for those lucky enough to be taking midwinter vacations. But you needn't be traveling to try one on and to be motivated by the pre-spring sight of yourself in a bikini or an even more formfitting 1-piece maillot. And with 5 months before the official start of summer, you'll be far ahead of everyone else with this early-bird diet strategy.

 Plan a seaside vacation to encourage you to diet into your swimsuit.

The prospect of having to wear a bathing suit is fabulous incentive for concentrating on your diet. Schedule the trip far enough in advance to see results but not so far that you put off dieting or have time to get lax about it: Within 3 to 6 months from now is a good time frame.

```
┌─·──·─┐
│ TIP  │  **Slenderize your sense of style.**
│ #233 │
└──────┘  Treat yourself to up-to-the-minute fashion mag-
```
azines instead of those on cooking and housekeeping.
Interesting fashion spreads and image-boosting articles
will revitalize you and renew your morale for dieting.

```
┌─·──·─┐
│ TIP  │  **Use dieter's logic to motivate you.**
│ #234 │
└──────┘  Here's one example of the way you need to
```
change your thinking. The next time you're feeling de-
pressed, tell yourself that being fat is depressing but being
on a diet is positive. Then congratulate yourself on this
positive action.

```
┌─·──·─┐
│ TIP  │  **Sacrifice on the side of good**
│ #235 │  **looks.**
└──────┘
```

Next time you reach for a slice of pizza, consider all you'll
be giving up for that one minute's consumption:

- the compliments you've been hearing;
- being able to shop from the smaller size racks at
  your favorite stores;
- the surprise and double take as you catch sight of
  yourself in a mirror.

No, it's not worth it!

Put the stress of dieting into perspective with relaxation techniques.

TIP #236

Transcendental meditation, Zen, and even the exercise discipline of yoga are excellent forms of release. The basis of each of these philosophies lies in the proper breathing technique. Whether at home with your bedroom door closed or at the office with phones ringing and typewriters clicking away, you can do this easy exercise:

> Close your eyes and focus on your breathing. Listen to the rhythmic beating of your heart and concentrate on the exchange of oxygen through your nose and lungs. Block out all external influences and follow the flow of air through your body to draw into yourself. Feel all the tension leave your body with each breath. Continue to concentrate for 5 full minutes. Then open your eyes and feel renewed calm.

Use this technique for any kind of stress, be it related to the diet or any other of life's pressures.

Once a month review the entries in your journal to boost your motivation.

TIP #237

Keeping a journal helps your diet (see tip #9); reviewing the progress you've made by looking through weeks of entries helps keep you on your diet. You are reminded of the important strides you've made and gain the self-confidence most dieters are short on.

TIP #238 Keep a "thin" closet.

Do not allow yourself to spend a lot of money fleshing out a large-size wardrobe. Limit yourself to one special occasion outfit, such as a pair of black gabardine pants and a cobalt blue silk blouse. If you know that you have only one fashion "look" in your closet, your fashion sense will push you to keep losing weight.

TIP #239 To lift your spirits with proof of your hard work, try on your large-size outfit once a week as you lose weight.

There's nothing like the feeling of "fat clothes" swimming on your trimmed body and knowing that you don't have to wear them anymore.

TIP #240 To pamper your senses, set a special dinner table for yourself once a week.

Whether or not you include others is up to you, but you are the "guest of honor" at this event. Be sure to use your best china, crystal, and silverware. Candles and flowers make it extra nice. Soft lighting and music complete the picture. Celebrate eating smart.

TIP #241

When your morale needs a boost, energize yourself with exercise.

Try this 2-minute refresher any time you need to get your blood pumping and your spirits rising.

1. Stand straight with your feet a comfortable 12 inches apart. Bring both arms out to the sides up to shoulder level. Without moving the arms, press your shoulder blades in toward the spine (this takes pressure off the back).
2. In this position, rotate your arms clockwise 8 times. Then reverse, rotating counterclockwise 8 times. Repeat in both directions with each of these hand variations: closed fists; palms up with fingers pointing toward the ceiling; palms down with fingers pointing toward the floor. The entire series should take about 30 seconds.
3. Lower your arms to your sides.
4. Rest for 1 full minute with your eyes closed. Feel the stimulation in your upper body.
5. Jog in place for 30 seconds, lifting each knee as high as you can. For added calorie burning, you may repeat the arm sequence as you jog.

TIP #242

Rediscover the jump rope, an adult way to get over mood swings.

When you feel yourself getting grouchy from whipped-cream withdrawal, try 5 minutes of this high-powered aerobic exercise. Provided you already have sneakers, your total investment will be around $3. Jumping starts your adrenaline flowing, perks you up, relieves tension, and, most important, burns calories to speed weight loss.

Overcome dieter's blues by
TIP
#243 **calling a successful dieter for a**
pep talk.

When you start to wonder if the sacrifice is really worth it, when you start thinking about assembling the ingredients for Grandma's 7-layer Viennese torte, make a club soda date with someone who's "been there." A successful dieter knows the pain, the aggravation, the solitude that comes from separating yourself from the foods you love; he or she will know how to cheer you on by sharing personal experiences that will renew your motivation.

 When you are feeling depressed
TIP
#244 **and nothing you do helps, give in**
to the black mood... for 1 hour.

(Set your alarm clock!) Even a good cry is okay. Just don't bury yourself in hot fudge—depression is an emotional, not an eating, experience. Then at the end of the hour, motivate yourself emotionally by getting physical. The mind often follows the body's lead—when you feel run-down, you start to think run-down. More positively, when you get your body moving, your mind becomes more active as well. So take a walk around the block, go to the library, or just to the cleaners to drop off a suit if there's nothing in particular you want to do. Once outdoors, you'll start feeling renewed and energized... and find yourself wanting to browse in a favorite store or take a jog around the park.

Get in touch with your anxieties about becoming a thin person.

TIP #245

Very powerful subconscious influences are often the reason we fail on a diet. Deep down, you might be afraid of being thin—Will you be liked? Will your aspirations come true?—and might secretly sabotage your own efforts out of fear. One dieter on our panel came within 10 pounds of her goal twice: Because of her anxieties, she couldn't bring herself to reach it. She knew who she was as a heavy person; she was afraid of what life would be like thin. But she found the strength to confront those fears and to assuage them. She wrote out a list and answered each one. Once she realized she could cope with whatever came her way and that it had to be easier being thin, she gave herself one last push and lost those 10 pounds.

 Ignore all well-meaning but misinformed friends and relatives who insist on telling you you don't need to diet.

TIP #246

They either are fat themselves or haven't seen you nude! Talk back if you have to, but always know your own goals and don't let anyone deter you with flattery—there will be plenty of time for that later on.

TIP #247
Resist buying smaller-sized clothes as incentives to dieting.

No matter how tempting an apparel item might be, even if it's on sale, keep from talking yourself into it with promises such as "I just know 10 pounds from now it'll fit." The problem isn't with losing the weight; it's whether or not the style of the garment will flatter your body shape when thin. What you can do to keep your motivation high is keep a list of those clothes you'd like to try on when you reach your goal—you might even collect clippings from magazines or catalogs and "browse" through this scrapbook whenever you need to remind yourself of this great fringe benefit of your diligence.

TIP #248
Avoid turning to food for comfort.

It's no secret that being upset often leads us to seek the comfort of a favorite food. But food isn't an answer. Take a step away from the fridge and toward a real solution to the problem confronting you. Example: You are anxious about a new romantic interest and are driving yourself crazy waiting for the phone to ring; take the initiative and do the phoning yourself—positive action.

Swear off talking about your diet for the next 24 hours.

Dieting often comes with built-in depression. Cure? Stop thinking, talking, and breathing diet. Do not mention the word to anyone for 1 full day. If someone asks you about it, say it's going fine and move to another topic immediately. Don't quit the diet, just quit letting it dominate you.

CHAPTER 9

Developing Willpower

HOW TO RESIST TEMPTATION

Willpower is the inner voice that keeps you on the right track. These tips help you create it in 3 different ways: through appetite control (learning to distinguish between eating and overeating, between hunger and habit); through learning to resist temptation; by breaking the special attachment that exists between you and the act of eating.

You have more control over your body than any other aspect of your life—exert it!

TIP #250

Stop telling yourself that you have no self-control and start believing in yourself and your ability to reach your goal—only you can make the difference. Start each day by looking in the mirror and saying out loud, "Today I will control what I eat." Repeat this for 1 full minute, until you can "taste" your determination. And if you should feel tempted during the day, close your eyes and see yourself standing in front of the mirror to recall the feeling of control. Remember no one can lose the weight for you: You must make your diet work.

Learn to recognize signs of hunger.

These include stomach pangs and grumblings; a feeling of light-headedness; the sensation of needing food. When you're genuinely hungry, you're likely to accept any food; a particular craving usually means you want to eat out of habit instead of need and should be squelched. Once you are adept at distinguishing hunger, you will find it much easier to curb your intake of food.

Teach yourself to stop eating for the wrong reasons.

Most people overeat because of 3 overriding impulses:

- Habit, such as raiding the cookie jar as soon as you get home.
- Boredom, such as making a grilled cheese sandwich because there's nothing good on TV.
- Stress. That's the hand that reaches for the peanuts as you work through the night to meet a deadline.

To break these patterns, find replacements:

- Head for the shower not the kitchen after a long day's work.
- Reach for a novel when you're bored with the usual TV fare.
- Keep plenty of no-calorie beverages handy to sip when you're on overtime.

To develop willpower, give yourself a visual choice to make when a craving strikes.

TIP #253

Tempted to eat a rich and gooey slice of pecan pie? Pick up a magazine instead. Find 2 photographs: an appetizing food dish and a fabulous fashion layout. Then ask yourself what you want more, the food or to look model-terrific in those clothes? Take the time to consider the alternatives—a moment of oral satisfaction or a future of good looks. If the answer isn't strong enough to satisfy the food urge, close your eyes and imagine yourself wearing the beautiful fashions; concentrate on the image and your craving will subside.

 ## To strengthen your resolve, show off your willpower.

TIP #254

Example: When your coworkers are lining up at the pastry-and-coffee cart, say loudly enough for all to hear, "None for me today." In addition to saving yourself tasteless calories (think of how stale baked goods get riding up and down the elevator all day!), you will hear oohs, ahhs, and praise for your sacrifice. And that will, in turn, keep you from sneaking a danish later on!

 ## Reward yourself for your willpower.

TIP #255

Congratulate every food sacrifice you make by treating yourself to a nonfood substitute. Splurge on a cab if you passed on the sautéed potatoes. Use the $3 dessert you skipped when out to dinner to have a blouse dry-cleaned rather than hand-washing it. Buy a new set of sheets if you swear off ice cream for 6 weeks. Work on the brownie-point system, using this exchange plan as a guide:

If you pass up	you earn	When you save up	you splurge on
1 chocolate chip cookie	5 points	30 points	four padded hangers
1 creamed soup	10 points	45 points	bath gel and lotion
1 junk-food dinner	20 points	60 points	a bangle bracelet
1 ice cream sundae	35 points	75 points	a silk teddy

By treating yourself to life's other pleasures, you will stop viewing food as a reward and will need it less.

Learn to say no.

TIP #256

The problem isn't that you don't know the word but that you don't use it often enough! Practice it in front of a mirror or with a friend until you can comfortably say it to yourself, to a persistent waiter, even to those relatives who think you're too thin! Saying no is the only way to keep that chocolate mousse pie out of your mouth.

Be prepared with excuses when saying no isn't enough.

TIP #257

When you're faced with a determined host or hostess who insists on waving the tempting hors d'oeuvre tray under your nose and asks "Why not?" offer one of these excuses as you turn down the appetizer:

- "I'm allergic to it—I break out in giant hives."
- "I've had one already—delicious!"
- "I can't—I have high blood metabolism" or make up your own incurable ailment!

Make the living room, not the kitchen, your home's social center.

Part of changing eating patterns is separating yourself from food. Let friends know they should come by the front door instead of the kitchen and entertain in the living room or den to put some distance between you and temptation.

 Find a private retreat in your home, one you can escape to when family members go on a binge by the TV.

For those times when not even your ironclad willpower can withstand everyone else's munching away, sequester yourself in your own sanctuary, away from the Goobers and peanut brittle. This can be your bathroom (spend 30 minutes pampering yourself in the tub), your den or spare room (where you can read a romance without any distractions), even your bedroom—just close the door to temporarily block out the world.

 When you're at home, switch from the TV to the radio for "companionship."

TV commercials are brutal—stylists make the food ads look irresistible and make the temptation for you to keep running to the fridge irresistible too! Try tuning into the radio for real "background" music: fewer food commercials and no visuals!

TIP #261 **Develop your sense of smell to control your sense of taste.**

The next time you crave a donut, visit your nearby bakery (leave your wallet at home!). As you walk into the store, inhale the aroma. As you pretend to browse, breathe deeply, at least 6 times—equivalent to the number of bites it would take to eat a donut. Get your fill of the aroma and then leave, as though nothing interested you. This kind of fix can, with practice, not only get rid of hunger pangs but also teach you to be satisfied without having to taste. And who knows, someday you might even be able to do it with money in your pocket!

 TIP #262 **To break the habit of needing a sweet after a meal, start by saying no to coffee.**

Coffee and cake is a natural reflex; for dessert addicts, the smell and the taste of coffee trigger the added desire for something sweet to go along with it. Learn to end a meal with a palate-cleansing glass of water. Note: If coffee in the morning means a sweet roll, substitute half a grapefruit to change your A.M. pattern.

 TIP #263 **Curb a sugar craving by eating a sour pickle.**

The fastest way to stop the desire for 1 of the 4 tastes (salt, sweet, sour, bitter) is to counter with 1 of the others. A sour pickle, at 15 calories, does the trick every time you think you want a piece of cake or pie. Keep a jarful on hand—pickles make a great snack anytime.

TIP #264 Pinpoint your snacking pattern and then work to break it.

Jot down those times during the day when you feel a strong need to munch. In a week's time, take an overview to determine your particular witching hours and schedule constructive activities at these times to otherwise occupy yourself. Example: If 5:45 P.M. is a targeted trouble time, schedule housecleaning or dog walking at that hour; if 2 A.M. finds you on a beaten path to the fridge, turn toward the TV instead and pick up on whatever old feature film is airing. Make a conscious effort to break the snack habit, and within a few weeks, you will have gained control over one of the chief causes of overweight.

 TIP #265 Stop making excuses for keeping snack foods in the house.

"It's for the kids" and "In case company drops in" are two familiar phrases that are really coverups for your wanting snacks handy and available. You're really fooling only yourself. Try a coffee-table fruit bowl as a substitute for bridge mix, mixed nuts, and the like; it will satisfy you, the kids, and the most discriminating guest, too.

TIP #266 It's svelter to give than to receive!

When you get a high-calorie food gift (a Christmas fruitcake, Valentine chocolates, and the like), give it away immediately. Find a friend, a colleague, a doorman or mail carrier who will be delighted to help keep you on your diet. Remember, if it's not in the house, you can't eat it!

TIP #267 To become less dependent on food, try to eat in the company of others.

For those who love eating, food is more than sustenance; it becomes a special "friend." To break this fattening relationship, work to put the importance of food back into perspective. Eating in front of others—spouse, friends, coworkers—helps diminish the forbidden allure of food and makes you more able to control quantity. One dieter relished eating cookies and liked savoring them in private—often consuming 3 or 4 times as many as she should have. By simply learning to eat them at the dinner table, with her family, she was able to break the high-cal fascination they held and to consume them as a regular food item rather than a precious treat.

TIP #268 Resist eating to please others.

Example: You arrive at your aunt's for dinner and find that though you told her about your diet in advance, she has gone ahead and prepared a lavish, high-cal dinner and you feel obliged to eat it. Don't. No matter how strong a motivator guilt is, do not give in. Limit yourself to the amount of food your diet allows and compliment her profusely, but don't ask for more, nor for leftovers. Remember that you can always explain your reasons for dieting and for not breaking your diet; if the other person cares for you, he or she will understand.

TIP #269

Be prepared for weak moments with a list of alternatives to food.

When you just can't seem to get your mind off food, try one or more of the following to refocus your outlook:

- Call a very gossipy friend and have a long chat.
- Develop a hobby or craft you've always wanted to pick up, one that's always handy.
- Become involved in a long-range project that calls for a lot of your time, such as joining a local theater group; organizing fund-raising events for a special charity; publishing a house organ.

TIP #270

If you work at home and are used to hourly eating, use low-cal beverages to shorten between-meal intervals.

Jazz up water with slices of lime; add the juice of half a lemon and 1 teaspoon of honey to hot water for a variation on the tea theme; make low-cal lemonade using club soda, the juice of a lemon, and Equal® for sweetness. These are all great appetite subduers that help break the nonstop eating pattern that plagues many homeworkers.

To cope with hunger on the job, keep a Things to Do list on your desk.

Itemize those office projects you've been putting off, from letters that need to be written to overdue memos to filing that's been piling up in the corner of your executive suite to back-burner assignments you vow to get to "someday." Whenever you feel like eating unscheduled food, tackle the first thing on your list. Cross off items as they are accomplished; add new ones as they come up. At the end of your diet, you'll have lost not only your extra weight but your gift for procrastination as well.

 Stave off false hunger pangs with a deep breath.

This painless "exercise" banishes those tummy twinges by relaxing abdominal muscles. Do it whenever you feel the urge to eat in between meals.

1. Lie flat on your back, legs straight out in front of you slightly apart. Let your body go limp; do not hold it rigid.
2. Place your hands on your abdomen and spread fingers wide apart, like two starfish.
3. Inhale, ballooning your stomach outward. At the same time, use your fingertips and the palms of your hands to resist this, as though you were trying to keep your tummy down. Breathe in as much air as your lungs can hold.
4. Slowly exhale, allowing the pressure from your hands to deflate your stomach.
5. Repeat the inhalation-exhalation 10 times to fully curb the urge to eat.

Use herbal tea "aromatherapy" to

TIP
#273

satisfy your appetite.

Fragrant herbal teas are an excellent way of suppressing hunger and fooling yourself into feeling full. The more exotic blends, such as apple blossom, mandarin orange and spice, cinnamon and rose hips, and lemon mint, are delicious enough to savor without added sugar or even a substitute and are minus the caffeine of regular teas and coffee. Be sure to inhale the aroma as you sip the tea to make the beverage even more satisfying. Note: In warm months, herbal teas are terrific when iced.

 At home, have a tray of juice

TIP
#274

cubes in the freezer to pop as a 10-calorie snack.

Freeze a variety of juices in the compartments of an ice-cube tray—any or all of your favorites. When you need to satisfy an oral craving, just pop 1 out of the tray and into your mouth! In addition to the pacifying effect of sucking on the cube, the cold dulls your tastebuds, reducing your desire for food.

Keep your pocket money green.

TIP
#275

Get out of the habit of carrying loose change for the office vending machine or a quick candy fix at the corner newsstand. Most of us are reluctant to break large bills for these items, so be sure to carry bills only, preferably higher than $5.

Pack your own popcorn.

TIP #276

When going to the movies, a concert, or a sporting event, bring your own legal munch to satisfy yourself while everyone else indulges at the concession counter. You won't feel deprived or tempted off your diet if you have your own snack. And to be on the safe side, don't carry any extra candy or soda money with you—this is vitally important if you are the type of spectator who usually loads up out of habit before you even find your seat!

When the peanuts are being passed at a party, take a powder!

TIP #277

A trip to the powder room, that is. Physically removing yourself from temptation is a surefire way to resist it.

Should you go "off" your diet, stop eating as soon as you can.

TIP #278

The rationale of those who pig out is often "Since I've blown it, I might as well eat all I want." Wrong! Say you go off your diet by eating a dish of ravioli. If you stop yourself after that dish, you can call it a maintenance day—no weight loss but, more important, no weight gain. But if you keep on eating more and more ravioli, well, that's a different story: serious backtracking. Get back on track after as little damage as possible.

TIP #279

Think of dieting as a balancing act: You might lose your equilibrium every now and then, but you always return to your center.

After a break in your diet, such as a binge, resume your menu plan by eating your usual number of daily meals. Resist the urge to skip a few meals—2 wrongs that don't make a right. The best way for your body to return to its normal digestive pattern is with your usual number of meals and calories. Rather than boosting weight loss, irregular eating slows your metabolism making the loss harder and longer to achieve.

TIP #280

On the day after a binge, opt for an all-fruit day.

To get you back to healthy eating and to help cleanse your system without resorting to extreme measures (see the previous tip), satisfy your portion intake with *fresh* fruit, any variety or combination that adds up to your caloric total. *You should consult your physician before doing this.*

CHAPTER 10

Support Systems

HOW TO ENLIST THE AID OF OTHERS

Going it alone is hard. It's hard to be "good" if everyone around you is enjoying food and you can't. You need support from all sides—friends, family, coworkers, other dieters. These tips show you how to get the cooperation and understanding you need for continued success.

Find a dieting "buddy."

TIP #281

Tell one special someone—a fellow dieter—about your diet. The buddy system was never as supportive as when applied to struggling dieters. Set up a panic line between your two homes and/or offices. Know each other's weak moments (when the afternoon coffee trolley rolls into friend Bev's office, when your grandfather clock strikes 11 P.M.) and arrange to call or to be called when these occur. If you know your buddy will be phoning to ask if you can resist a snack attack, your motivation will be higher. Sometimes just knowing that there's a reassuring voice at the other end of the phone can help you deal with a food crisis without your even having to make the call.

TIP #282

When you and your spouse are both dieting, you need to provide motivation for each other.

Success comes from teamwork: Recognize that you both won't always feel motivated at the same time; some days, you will take the role of leader to get you both to the gym; on other days, your spouse will be the one to say "Put those brownies back on the shelf." Promise each other that when one is feeling lax, the other will step in rather than encourage the laxness. When each works for the other, both achieve success.

 TIP #283

When you and your spouse diet together, find an at-home activity you can both enjoy and turn to when dieter's irritability strikes after dinner.

Here are just a few examples:

- Rent a VCR and have your own '30s movies revival or a Burt Reynolds film festival—rent a different movie for each night of the week.
- Become amateur astrologers with a telescope for stargazing.
- Rediscover the mystery and take turns reading to each other from the volumes of Ellery Queen, Agatha Christie, and *The Adventures of Sherlock Holmes*, by Arthur Conan Doyle.

To rally your family to your side, discuss your diet goals with your kids.

TIP
#284

Explain that you need their cooperation, that sweets will be restricted because they tempt you, that there won't be any special orders while you're on the diet—unless they can prepare them themselves. Do make your snacks available to them—fresh fruit, yogurt, raisins, and the like —when they get hungry. Teaching them good nutrition principles can help them prevent overweight, too.

 When you're dieting and trying to satisfy a growing family at the same time, recruit all home members to aid in meal planning.

TIP
#285

Trying to figure out 3 menus a day is hard enough when you're on a strict weight loss plan—composing 3 others for nondieting spouse and kids can drive you crazy. Since part of dieting is limiting the amount of time you think about food, getting some input from your family is an invaluable diet aid. Set aside 1 hour a week during which you can draw up a master list and schedule.

To help keep you from being tempted, enlist your family's aid in the kitchen.

TIP #286

The less you must be around food, the easier it is to curb your desires. If you're like most dieters with a family, you're fine during the daytime. But when it comes to cooking for a group in the evening, willpower starts weakening. By getting assistance from your spouse and children, you can keep your willpower running strong. Delegate responsibility: Spouse makes the salad, kid #1 sections the grapefruit; kid #2 washes the veggies, and you broil the turkey burgers. Once you let your family act as your own private support group, you'll find dinnertime a breeze.

 ## Dole out each family member's portions in the kitchen.

TIP #287

Avoid serving meals "family style," with large bowls and platters centered on your table. These are tempters and encourage overindulging (they also make extra cleanup work!).

 ## Put other family members in charge of clearing the table on a rotational basis.

TIP #288

Not having to deal with the dishes means not being tempted to put those 3 leftover forkfuls of your son's mashed potatoes into your awaiting mouth! Ask the table clearers to put these smidgens in the trash and to store any substantial portions in labeled containers.

TIP #289

When you and your family are all trying to lose weight, explain the motivation drive to your kids to encourage them to stick with your weight loss plan.

Though your children might be devastated by the cut in the Mars-bar supply, they will be even more hurt by peer pressure if they are chubby. Helping them understand why dieting is necessary will make their sacrifices easier. One of the best ways to get their minds off food is with after-school clubs and activities you can participate in, too—with eager enthusiasm, candy and soda will take second or even third place!

TIP #290

Ask for support from your coworkers.

One of our dieters found it impossible to be faithful to her weight loss program because of an office mate who believed in starting the day with hot cross buns—enough for everyone. Another dieter worked in a very large office where each week brought a birthday celebration for someone or other. Both found that by letting their coworkers know about their diet and susceptibility to temptation, their colleagues were more than happy to help. Dieter #1's problem was solved by the office mate's eating her breakfast in the firm's lunchroom. Dieter #2 made it a point to be out of the office during the lunch hour when the birthday cake of the week was being served.

If you can't "go it alone," join a diet group.

TIP #291

Even if you have the best intentions toward taking responsibility for your overweight, you might need the support a group can give you. It is not a sign of weakness but one of strength, showing that you have the courage to stand up, admit your problem, and ask for help. A diet group offers a unique double-edged motivation: The recognition and praise you get from your peers will encourage you to stick with it; the potential for disappointing other members by not showing up at meetings will spur you on as well. Both work together for your success... at about $5 a visit!

 When selecting a diet center, look for one that offers the widest range of features.

TIP #292

These include:

- classes, lectures, and special events (one center in New York stays open on all the major holidays, when cravings can really ruin your motivation);
- flexible meeting hours to accommodate you and any other family members (if your kids are overweight, now is the time to help them as well as yourself!);
- behavior-modification techniques that teach you to replace food with activity;
- an arrangement with neighborhood restaurants to offer menus that adhere to the group's diet plan.

Avoid diet programs that require you to purchase prepackaged diet foods as part of their plan.

Many such businesses depend on these sales to stay afloat, subjecting you to needless limitations on your menu planning. An organization that offers various aids is fine; but one that forces them on you is not. Learning to deal with real foods is what will keep you thin.

 When you join a diet center, make yourself a strict promise of attendance.

Never miss or postpone a session: If you allow yourself to make an excuse 1 day, you'll find coming up with another (and another) one that much easier. To stay on track, plan your other engagements around this all-important appointment.

 When you begin membership at a diet center or group, attend 2 or 3 times a week, at least for the first 3 weeks.

If you need the reinforcement and supervision of a group, chances are you need it more than once a week. This might cost you more at first, but it will help the system work: Our dieters found that a large expenditure that brings results is worth a lot more than a small amount of money down the drain!

Think of your diet center or group as more than just a weigh-in.

TIP #296

The interaction with other members—sharing experiences, even frustrations over dieting—makes joining worthwhile. If your center offers an exercise plan along with counseling, think of it as an all-in-one stop for getting both your time and your money's worth.

CHAPTER 11

Charting Your Progress

HOW TO MEASURE RESULTS

A weight loss course is rarely swift and steady. There are plateaus, even setbacks that have to be dealt with. The tips in this chapter explain how you can make your weight loss goal seem more attainable and how to judge your progress in a variety of satisfying ways.

TIP #297 **Break down your total weight loss goal into more easily attained mini-goals.**

Set up 3 stages of accomplishment: half the total, then another quarter, then the final quarter. Losing a fraction at a time is more realistic and less insurmountable than facing the total head-on. As you reach each stage, take the time for a round of self-congratulations—but don't celebrate with a binge. (Note that the first stage is set at half because most dieters lose a disproportionately high amount of weight in the beginning.)

Set your weekly weight loss goal at 1 pound.

TIP #298

Although the first week or two of dieting often produces greater results in general, don't try to exceed this moderate loss. Rapid weight loss usually results from water loss and is always followed by rapid regains. The only way to keep weight off is to take it off slowly. Gradual weight loss also gives overstretched skin the time it needs to return to normal without falling into flabby-looking folds.

 If you rely on your scale as an indicator of weight loss, keep a daily chart to record your overall weight patterns.

TIP #299

Reviewing the chart over a period of a few months will tell you if there are certain times of each month when you tend to hit temporary water-weight plateaus. For women, these are most often linked to stages in the menstrual cycle and can occur just before, during, or after your period, or even midcycle. Knowing your slow days in advance can prevent unnecessary scale-oriented frustration.

Get into the habit of measuring your loss in inches as well as pounds.

Learn to use the tape measure as the most accurate gauge of body reshaping. This is especially important when you consider that healthy muscle gained from exercise weighs more than fat cells yet has less volume (muscle cells are more compact). The scale alone may not measure your full progress. Record your measurements on a separate page of your diet journal (see tip #9); measure upper arms, bust, waist, hips, upper thighs, and calves. Re-measure and chart every 2 to 4 weeks.

 Use photographs to visually chart your progress.

Ask someone close to you (preferably your diet buddy— see tip #281) to photograph you once a month. These "for your eyes only" pictures will give you proof-positive reinforcement that will keep you on track. Be sure to date the back of each print for accuracy. And whenever you feel blue or need a reminder of the strides you've made, take out your photos and show off to yourself.

 As you near your goal, be prepared for more frequent plateaus.

The more weight lost, the more your body tries to hold on to the weight it has been carrying. If you are aware of this natural tendency and can psych yourself in advance to ignore each plateau as it presents itself, you can avoid "plateau depression." To cope with the plateau when it arrives, follow the avoid-the-scale advice in the following tip and take out your private photos, described in tip #301.

If your scale shows no improvement over the course of 1 week, stop weighing yourself for 2 more weeks.

There's no need to watch that indicator not move, so stay away from it. The same dieter's logic applies to looking incessantly in the mirror: The more you look, the fatter you feel. After an "abstinence" of 3 weeks, you should see a change that will justify your sustained effort. Conversely, jumping on and off the scale every hour (as many dieters do in their frustration!) will only break it...and your spirit, too.

 When you're only 10 pounds from your goal, make every fourth week a maintenance one.

Keep calories down, but have foods in *slightly* greater quantity. This practice will prepare you for your new way of life and prevent the panic most dieters experience when they go off a diet and are on their own. You'll know from firsthand experience that you can keep that weight off for good!

 Set for yourself the goal of looking terrific.

When setting your ultimate weight loss objective, use your objectivity, as well as other indicators. Remember that 125 pounds at age 40 might not look the same as it did at age 22—the scale alone isn't enough of a gauge. Take a good look at yourself in a mirror, nude or in a bathing suit that used to fit you well. Then ask yourself if you've reached your goal.

CHAPTER 12

The Beauty, Health, and Style of Losing Weight

SATISFYING THE NEEDS OF A CHANGING BODY

Looking and feeling great as you diet provides you with the reinforcement you need to stick with it. As your beauty and fashion sense emerges, you'll feel renewed and motivated all over again. All these tips work to boost your appearance—the very thing that inspired you to diet in the first place.

TIP #306

Maximize your above-the-neck good looks to encourage your body to play catch-up.

Realize your full beauty potential by trying new makeup techniques and by experimenting with a new hairstyle—the latter for men *and* women. When you see how attractive your face can be, you'll feel more self-confident and more anxious to bring your body up to par. Remember that overweight need never mean unattractive.

TIP #307

The next time you need a morale boost, treat yourself to a manicure or a pedicure.

You needn't think that you have to be thin before you can treat yourself to such body pampering—everyone is entitled. And the more you take care of yourself, the more likely people will be to notice your assets instead of your size.

| TIP #308 | **Increase your diet savvy by wising up to the good health advantages of being thin.** |

Vanity is a prime motivator in the battle of the bulge but isn't the only one. Feeling good should count as much as looking good, and the way to accomplish both goals is to diet smart. To boost your nutrition knowledge, write to the Food and Drug Administration for up-to-the-minute pamphlets that make for interesting as well as educational reading. Two to ask for: *Weight Loss*—Dept. 81 and *Key to Nutrition*—Dept. 598L. Address: Consumer Information Center, Pueblo, Colorado 81009.

| TIP #309 | **To stay pretty, stay healthy on your diet, eat no fewer than an average of 1000 calories a day.** |

If you eat too little, your health will suffer and you might develop serious beauty problems as well—skin breakouts and excessive hair loss are two common complaints. If after boosting your intake as suggested you are still experiencing these problems, check with your doctor to see if any vitamin or mineral deficiencies could be the cause.

| TIP #310 | **To stay pretty while dieting, use creams or body lotions to counter the dryness that often results from reduced fat intake.** |

Cutting out butter and oils from your diet does help in your weight loss efforts but can contribute to the unpleasant side effect of dry skin. Using vitamin E–or aloe vera–based lotion for the body and moisturizer on the face (under the eyes especially) will keep your skin moist and soft to the touch.

TIP #311

To reduce water weight and bloating, both frustrating to the dieter, reduce your salt intake.

By keeping sodium levels down, you help reduce health risks and eliminate extra body fluids. Avoid adding salt when you cook; avoid buying packaged goods that contain salt; and use it minimally, if at all, at the table.

TIP #312

To alleviate the discomfort of constipation, a frequent complaint among dieters, try this natural "remedy."

1. From a standing position, bend your knees and, with a straight back, lower yourself to a squatting position.
2. Lean your upper body forward until your hands can touch the floor in front of you. Your weight should be balanced between your hands and the balls of your feet (your heels and buttocks do not touch the floor).
3. Hold this position for 3 to 5 minutes to put gentle pressure on your bowels. Slowly stand up.
4. Follow this by drinking a glass of warm water mixed with the juice of half a lemon, a natural laxative.
   Within 2 hours, the constipation should be relieved.

1. Bend your knees to lower yourself...

2. ...to a squat position.

3. Balance on your hands and the balls of your feet for up to five minutes...

4. ...then slowly lift yourself to a standing position and follow with the rest of the tip.

Treat weight loss "symptoms" with smarts, not food.

TIP #313

Frequently dieters develop psychosomatic illnesses that can scare you off your diet or lead you to seek a remedy in food. If either (or both!) of these ailments attacks you, treat them with the following healthful suggestions:

- Headaches: Take an aspirin substitute and resist thinking "I must be eating too little food."
- Dizziness: Take a few seconds longer when rising from a seated or prone position and resist thinking "I must be eating too little food."

Regardless of your clothing size, start thinking of your fashion image right now.

TIP #314

Shop for complete outfits: All the separates (such as a shirt, pants, and jacket or sweater) needed to create a total fashion "look." The only thing that looks and feels worse than clothes haphazardly thrown together are large-size clothes haphazardly thrown together!

Have ready at all times one wear-anywhere outfit in which you feel good.

TIP #315

If you don't feel that you look good in your clothes, you won't feel motivated to get out of the house and get involved. But if you know that you are comfortable in a pair of well-fitting jeans and an oversized shirt or in a soft-hued smock, you will be able to get yourself out of the sedentary pattern that encourages overweight.

When shopping for clothes while still losing weight, select styles that can adapt as your size changes.

TIP #316

Buy pants and skirts with adjustable waistlines, such as drawstring closures and elasticized waistbands. Smock blouses and tent dresses can be "trimmed" with a belt. Jeans and fancy sweats—activewear—can often be gently shrunk in the washer and dryer unless they specify Dry-clean Only.

Buy fewer, better-made clothes.

TIP #317

The better the garment, the more carefully and fully it will be cut and the better it looks on you. And because of its superior craftsmanship, the easier it will be to take in as you get skinny. One more psychological advantage: Because of the cut, you will be able to select a smaller size. It's the fastest way for a size 20 to become a size 16!

TIP #318 **As you lose weight, shop for clothes that enhance your emerging body type.**

Wearing baggy, shapeless garments actually calls more attention to a weight problem. Determine your figure assets and dress to highlight them instead. Examples: Women should show off slim calves with shorter, knee-length skirts or culottes. If you have a small waist, accentuate it with a wide belt. Strapless dresses and jumpsuits are great if you have slim arms and shoulders. Close-fitting pants worn with an oversized blouson are fashionable if you have good hips and legs yet need to camouflage a heavy abdomen or upper body. Men who carry extra weight in their stomachs should avoid clingy polo-type shirts. Cotton shirts and loose sweaters are more stylish worn over pants, not tucked inside. And a navy blazer always adds Cary Grant allure as the dark color slims the silhouette.

 TIP #319 **Don't try squeezing into the smallest possible size.**

If you're caught between 2 sizes, one a bit tight, the other a bit loose, buy the looser item. First, you'll feel comfortable when you wear it (one of the worst things about being heavy is feeling uncomfortable in everything!). Second, the sensation of loose clothing is a sign of weight loss success, so psychologically your spirits will be better. Third, you'll look great—tight clothes make even a thin person look fat and unattractive.

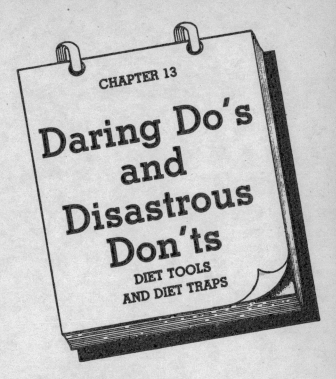

CHAPTER 13

Daring Do's and Disastrous Don'ts

DIET TOOLS AND DIET TRAPS

The "Do's" are a roundup of the most unconventional tips our diet panel listed; they are included here because, though they are unusual, they really did make an effective difference. They're offered for your consideration.

The "Don'ts" are diet traps that were found not only to impede your progress (though most boasted just the opposite!) but also to be potentially dangerous to your health.

Do... curb your desire to eat by tightening your belt... literally.

TIP #320

Studies (and our test panel) have shown that tightening your belt 1 notch before a meal helps contract tummy muscles, making you feel full earlier. Wearing slightly tight pants is a viable alternative, preventing your stomach from expanding, which, in turn, prevents you from overeating.

Do... break the tasting habit as you cook, by wearing a painter's mask.

TIP #321

Tasting is a reflex for most cooks—you might not even realize how often you do it—but those calories add up. This device, though somewhat unusual, helps you break the habit by first making you conscious of it. Not only does the mask put a barricade between you and your spoon; it also helps block out aromas that can tempt you. Saving yourself these taste-test calories can add up to extra pounds lost with the help of one tip alone!

 Do... have your refrigerator fitted with a time lock if you are very weak-willed.

TIP #322

This will make it impenetrable from the moment you set it in the evening to the time you designate the next morning. Drastic—but it works.

 Do... become aware of how unattractive overeating is by watching yourself in a mirror.

TIP #323

Most dieters are so absorbed by the food they are consuming that they aren't conscious of the image they project to others. The next time you have a meal, set a mirror on your dining room table and observe yourself in action. Your sense of vanity will cause you not only to slow down but to eat less, too.

Do...use "shock therapy" to keep yourself on the diet track with the help of your mirror.

TIP #324

Put on underwear and knee socks and stand in front of a full-length mirror. These particular garments "cut" your body into unflattering angles, making it impossible for any flab to go unnoticed: One look and you'll be shocked back onto your diet, should you think of straying.

Do...acknowledge chocoholism—and work with it.

TIP #325

Chocolate is a problem food in a class by itself. The idea of chocolate denial is so unthinkable to a true chocoholic that dieting seems impossible. Well, it doesn't have to be that way. You may include it on whatever diet you're on, as long as you learn to control it. Limit yourself to 1 ounce (145 calories) a day in whatever form you like, eliminating an equivalent number of calories from other food sources— alcohol, butter or oils, or nuts are ideal because you aren't sacrificing many nutrients.

Do...replace a high-calorie hard candy habit by sucking on a clove.

TIP #326

This delicious spice makes a fantastic no-calorie substitute that satisfies the oral cravings that plague most dieters. Just pop one in your mouth and gently bite into it periodically to release some of its powerful essence. It also freshens "dieter's breath." Be sure to carry a few in a Baggie at all times.

Do... burn off extra calories by turning down the thermostat at home and in the office!

To maintain its ideal internal temperature of 98.6, the body will burn more energy when its environment is on the cool side. Of course, you don't want to freeze, but do keep a nip in the air. And remember that doing 25 easy jumping jacks will warm you up as much as a sweater and burns off even more calories!

 Do... turn to comedy as a mood lifter when dieter's irritability lands you in the dumper.

Celebrated editor and essayist Norman Cousins believed comedy helped cure his paralyzing illness; medical studies prompted by his theory confirm the positive effects of laughter. Comedy can take you out of yourself and leave you feeling very up. Go to a Woody Allen film festival; a comedy club on amateur night; the record store for a comedy album; or the video shop for your favorite comedian's tape. Don't feel like leaving the house? Turn on cartoons, vintage Merry Melodies and Loonytunes—a daily dose makes for great "preventive medicine."

 Do... send yourself subliminal "thin" messages via your TV and home computer.

Stimutech's video cartridges, available at your video store, flash diet-boosting messages on your TV screen for a fraction of a second. Those such as "I will be thin" and "I look slender" are too fast for the eye to see but appear long enough for the brain to register. Not all the scientific data is in concerning the effectiveness of this approach, but coupled with some positive thinking, it just might help boost your motivation.

Do...go to sleep when you can't fight hunger anymore!

This at-home solution works—and gets you the extra sleep you need if you're on an exercise program, too. Just a 15-minute catnap is enough to break the hunger cycle. And you'll use up 15 calories instead of ingesting countless more.

 Don't follow any diet that promises a loss of 10 pounds in 10 days, 7 pounds in 7 days; 14 pounds in 14 days...Impossible!

Unless you spend 10 hours each of those days skiing and eat under 500 calories. (Not a very practical idea if you live in the Sun Belt!) We know you're tempted, but don't think that the results of such plans will live up to your expectations.

TIP #332 **Don't buy another fad diet book; shop for an informative nutrition guide instead.**

You'll learn about the vital role food plays in keeping you alive and well, and you'll soon find yourself wanting to build a lifelong "diet" around those nutrients that encourage your best health.

Don't get into the "diet pill" habit.

TIP #333 No matter how many manufacturers insist their over-the-counter diet pills are safe, they shouldn't be considered as an effective diet aid. If you learn to rely on them to suppress hunger for you, you may become dependent on them for the rest of your life—and many do have unpleasant side effects, such as irritability, nervousness, and insomnia, leaving you feeling high or "wired." It seems easier to pop a pill than to have to create your own willpower, but mastering your appetite on your own is really the only way to achieve permanent weight loss.

Don't try food substitutes in pill form, such as "vegetable tablets," a popular gimmick.

TIP #334

Manufacturers boast of these vegetable substitutes containing nutrients equivalent to eating pounds of fresh produce. Test studies have shown this is not the case, that the pills have precious little vegetable matter in them at all! Fads like these, aimed at the health-conscious dieter, are springing up all the time. To protect yourself, make this rule: Stick to natural food sources and vitamin/mineral supplements only.

Don't fall into the diet trap of an
TIP **all-protein diet.**
#335

Despite all that has been researched and written on the
subject of a well-balanced diet, many so-called experts
continue to push all-meat and meat-and-fat diets on the
public, insisting that you can eat all you want and still
lose weight! That is simply impossible. Yes, turkey is a
lean protein source that's good for you, but an excess of
it in your system will have the same effect as an excess
of any other food: It turns to fat. Maintain your basic food
groups diet (see tip #12).

 Don't rely on liquid supplement
TIP **diets.**
#336

Whether the supplement is the dangerous liquid protein
or any other meal-in-a-can variety, this type of weight
loss program does not teach you about meal planning or
controlling quantities once you are off the diet. And worse,
these drinks can be nutritionally deficient (not to mention
tasteless). Without the variety of whole foods, sticking to
a diet is much too difficult.

Don't let yourself fall into the trap of bulimia.

TIP #337

Bulimia is the medical term for an eating disorder that can include purposely throwing up after eating as a way of controlling your weight. How to throw up is a diet "tip" many young women are sharing with each other on high school and college campuses across the country. Unfortunately it is a very dangerous practice when done even once. If you have come to rely on this as a form of weight loss (or control), please seek medical attention right away, either by calling your family doctor or by contacting the National Association for Anorexia Nervosa and Associated Disorders, Highland Park, Illinois.

 Don't consider surgery as an aid to weight loss, unless you consider it as a last resort.

TIP #338

From tummy tucks to removing fat folds, to fat-suction techniques that aspirate fat cells, to stapling the stomach, medical procedures have been developed to cope with the problem of overweight. Magazines are filled with stories of successful operations that don't seem to call for willpower. But it is important to put all these into perspective. They are forms of surgery, some very major indeed. Before considering any one, give yourself one more chance to lose the weight on your own. Give your diet a fighting chance by applying all our advice to it: hard, yes, but you can have the results you want with your own effort. All of us who contributed to this book are proof of that!

CHAPTER 14

Staying Thin

KEEPING YOUR NEW FIGURE

Losing weight is only half the battle—keeping it off, that's how you win the war! This is the most neglected aspect of dieting but by far the most important, making the difference between having the body you want and playing the human yo-yo yet another time. You need to switch gears when you go on "maintenance." Think of it as phase-2 dieting—more food but more caution, too, to make certain that your new way of eating, and living, is permanent.

Reorient your thinking in terms of weight control.

TIP #339

Weight maintenance requires a new kind of psyching, because, unlike dieting, it is forever. Psych yourself by repeating 10 times every morning, "Today I will work at staying thin." This will be a permanent part of your life, but the reward of an attractive and healthy body is worth it.

 Think of maintenance as the second, lifelong phase of your diet with its own set of rules to follow.

TIP #340

Resist thinking of it as your chance to break free of restrictions; that will only move you backward not ahead. Keep practicing the behavior modification techniques that helped you when dieting. The bonus here is that you can eat larger portions.

TIP #341

Start seeing yourself as a thin person.

Though they lose weight, many dieters have a hard time believing that they are slim. They still gravitate to the larger size clothes racks, still wear camouflaging styles, still withdraw from social invitations because they still feel self-conscious. The transition period is a difficult one: It's hard to believe you have succeeded at dieting, especially if you have always been an on-again, off-again dieter. Try to make the mental effort to feel thin: Force yourself, if you must, to try new things. Each night, before bed, plan one "thin person" act for the next day and see it through; this can be anything from trying on a form-fitting dress to investigating a sport you weren't comfortable doing before: aim to be daring. With a conscious try, the mental part of your diet will be as effective as the physical part.

TIP #342

To gradually incorporate additional calories into your daily diet, start with a pre-maintenance plan.

Alternate a diet day with a weight-control day: Monday, Wednesday, Friday, and Sunday of your *first* maintenance week, eat at diet levels; Tuesday, Thursday, and Saturday, increase to a beginning maintenance level of 1400 calories.

Use a gradual approach to determine your ultimate maintenance calorie level.

TIP #343

Follow this 4-week plan to adjust to your new eating pattern after eating at pre-maintenance levels (see the previous tip).

- Week #1: 1400 calories a day;
- Week #2: 1600 calories a day;
- Week #3: if there has been no weight gain, 1750 calories a day;
- Week #4: if there has been no weight gain, 1850 calories a day.

In the coming weeks, add on 50 more calories until you reach 2000 calories a day for women, 2500 a day for men *unless you notice any weight gain*. This is an average maintenance level for moderately active people of average height and weight. A sedentary woman of 50 who stands 5 feet tall and weighs 105 pounds might not progress past the level of week #2; a very active woman of 50 standing at 5 feet 6 inches with large bone structure might need 2500 calories to maintain her new body. Take the time you need to determine this "magic" number most carefully.

 Keep a maintenance plan journal in which to list your menus.

TIP #344

This is a continuation of your diet journal (see tip #9), adjusted to this second phase of your overall plan. Though you have more leverage in meal planning, you should stay with the dieting techniques used during weight loss to help you adjust to your new weight. Using a journal helps keep you from reverting to the overeating patterns that caused your overweight.

Incorporate 2 of your top 10 "love" foods into your weekly maintenance menus.

Identify your favorite foods on a sheet of paper and then work them into your meal plan, 2 at a time. Continued controlled indulgences make lifelong calorie counting bearable . . . and life more fun in general!

 Keep counting calories.

If you can't or won't, you run the greatest risk of regaining your lost weight. On the other hand, if you continue to keep careful track of them, at your higher maintenance levels you can eat anything you want! The choice is yours.

 Teach yourself to be satisfied with "thin-person portions."

Staying thin means being able to regulate acceptable portion sizes of the high-calorie foods you like. This exercise teaches that control. Buy a quarter-pound of toffee, for instance. On each of 4 days, substitute a 1-ounce piece for 100 of your maintenance calories, such as a tablespoon of butter. This is your daily limit; enjoy it. Fight the desire to eat any more by telling yourself that in less than 24 hours you will be savoring another piece. This is a challenge—make no mistake about it—but it's one you can win. And once you can make that quarter-pound stretch over 4 days, you'll be able to control yourself around all temptation items—even around a full-pound box of toffee!

Have only 1 high-calorie dish per meal.

TIP
#348

If you follow this simple principle, you can enjoy good food without backtracking. Here are examples of its application:

- If you are having a luscious appetizer, such as coquilles St. Jacques, the rest of your dinner should be broiled chicken (no skin), steamed vegetables, and fresh fruit;
- if you are having a rich entrée, such as beef goulash with broad noodles, start with half a grapefruit and have low-cal ices for dessert;
- if you are having a sumptuous layer cake for dessert, have the grapefruit appetizer and the plain chicken as your first 2 courses.

Keep your kitchen set up for weight loss.

TIP
#349

To discourage the old patterns from returning, keep your food scale on the counter and continue to weigh everything; keep your cabinets and fridge stocked as before; continue to rely on aids like club soda and sugar substitute to save on calories that can then be applied to foods you like more. These little rules avoid the return of the lax frame of mind you had before dieting.

Continue your exercise plan.

TIP #350

Hopefully you feel as addicted to exercise as successful dieters usually are and won't want to stop. But if you are tired of your usual routine, take up a new discipline. The absolute minimum is 3 workouts a week—without sustained exercise, your body will revert to burning fewer calories and at a slower rate. Translated to food intake, that means you won't be able to eat as much as you'd like.

 To stay active, apply my rule of "constant motion."

TIP #351

If you can lie down, sit up; if you can sit up, stand up; if you can stand, walk around; if you can walk, run!

Weigh yourself and maintain your weight chart on a daily basis (if you don't already).

TIP #352

This is important to help you determine the number of calories you need to hold your new weight. Suppose you maintain 135 pounds for 10 days, then you gain a pound. Unless this is water-weight time, the scale indicates that you are eating an average of 350 calories a day too much:

$$\frac{1 \ pound \ (3500 \ calories)}{10 \ days} = 350.$$ You would then cut back your daily allotment by that amount. Conversely, if, after 10 days, you lost a pound, you would increase your daily intake by 350 calories.

TIP #353

If you like the discipline of a diet during the week, try a "5-days-on, 2-days-off" maintenance plan.

You eat diet portions Monday through Friday, saving the extra calories from maintenance for the weekends when you go "off." Example: Assuming that your maintenance level is 1600 calories a day, by eating only 1200 calories during the week, you would have an extra 1000 calories to consume each day of the weekend. This is a viable lifelong eating plan, especially apropos for those who save eating out for Saturday and Sunday.

 TIP #354

If in-between meal hunger is still a problem, keep your eating plan at 6 small meals a day:

breakfast/midmorning/lunch/midafternoon/dinner/evening snack. At other times, continue to rely on liquids to curb hunger pangs. Eating small meals is a healthful way of eating, but remember to plan ahead with carry-along snacks on days you won't be in easy access of food: Once you're used to mini-meals, your body will know it if you miss 1.

 TIP #355

If you lost weight through a diet center or community, plan refresher visits at strict intervals.

If you used counselor supervision as a weight loss tool, going on your own cold turkey could prove disastrous. To get the maintenance supervision you need, schedule an appointment every 2 weeks for the first 3 months; once a month for the next 6 months; then every other month for the following 6.

Treat yourself to an expensive and flattering outfit as incentive to keep your weight under control.

And pack off old "fat" clothes to Goodwill, a needy neighbor, or cold storage (if you aren't brave): Not having them around to fall back on will help keep you on your guard.

 As soon as you feel any new clothes fitting a bit snugly, go back on your diet for 1 week.

Don't wait until you absolutely can't zip those pants—use the first sign of tightness as a flashing red light to get you to curb your intake. Refuse to alter these clothes or to buy others in a larger size—that's giving in to your old ways.

 Master the art of moderation to maintain your weight loss.

If you can practice moderation—being satisfied with 1 chocolate kiss instead of the whole bag!—you don't have to forsake any of your favorite foods. But if envisioning a mountain of kisses at the end of your diet is what kept you on it, know that there is no mountain, only a narrow trail leading far ahead. Make a new deal with yourself: You may enjoy chocolate kisses with the catch that you can have only *1 a day* (each packs a whopping 50 calories, so be sure to let it m-e-l-t in your mouth!).

When your appetite does get the better of you, don't berate yourself for overeating.

TIP #359

Don't judge yourself too critically, either. Food is a powerful influence; at times it does win out. Your only recourse is to admit that you overindulged and to become more aware of what you are doing and why. Remember that you will always be subject to the boredom/habit/stress cycle that pushes you toward food (see tip #256), but that there will be more days ahead when you will win out. As long as you retain the upper hand most of the time, you will stay thin.

 When you go off your maintenance plan at binge levels, follow with 3 diet days.

TIP #360

Do this even if the scale doesn't show a weight gain. This "separation" from food will put you back in a moderation frame of mind. Note: Anytime that scale does show a gain, whether it is of 1, 2, or 5 pounds, start your diet immediately. Do not put it off for even 1 day.

After 2 successful months of maintenance, you may begin to rely less on your journal.

TIP #361

See tip #344. If after 2 months you have kept off all the lost weight, start using a calculator with a memory to keep a running total of calories ingested throughout the day. One dieter found how best to get used to the new system: As soon as you reach your maximum calorie level, regardless of how early in the day that might be, you stop eating. After a few days of reaching her total by 3 P.M., she got the hang of mentally spreading out her intake!

Diet in advance.

TIP #362

If you are planning a trip, or even a special evening, and don't want to wake up with a weight gain when it's over, take off up to 3 pounds in advance for the vacation, 1 pound for an evening's worth of splurge.

 Always be on the lookout for ways to cut calories and to make the most of the ones you are allowed.

TIP #363

Do this by investigating:

- new low-calorie substitutes for high-calorie foods;
- low-calorie recipes that appear in women's magazines and on the boxes of your packaged diet foods;
- subscribing to a health-oriented magazine, such as *American Health, Prevention*, or body-builder Joe Weider's *Shape*.

You must effect a life-style change to keep your weight off.

TIP #364

Some people have begun their new thin life by changing homes, jobs, even cities, and certainly their inactive way of life. On a smaller scale, if your problem is the corn muffin you see at the bakery you pass to get to the bus to work, make your life-style change a switch to the subway or the car pool—whatever it takes to break your old pattern of walking into the store and walking out with the muffin already in your mouth. Making a lot of these little adjustments starts you living thin. And keeps you that way!

TIP #365

Once a week, and whenever you feel the need for a boost, take out the list of things you hope to achieve as a thin person (see tip #228) and take action toward accomplishing everything you have written down.

ABOUT THE AUTHOR

Julie Davis is the author of more than thirty books, both novels and self-help titles, including the international bestseller *30 Days to a Beautiful Bottom*. Julie's work has been translated into a total of fourteen foreign languages and has appeared in all the major women's magazines. She is a lecturer, a beauty consultant, and a popular talk-show guest. She is currently developing her own show for cable television. She lives in New York City with her husband, Charles Goldstein.

The food you eat can save your life...

Available at your bookstore or use this coupon.

____ **CRAIG CLAIBORNE'S GOURMET DIET, Craig Claiborne**   29579   2.95
A program you can easily follow, day after day, year after year, for the rest of your life...
contains 200 specially created, low sodium, modified fat recipes.

____ **AMERICAN HEART ASSOCIATION COOKBOOK**
Ruthe Eshleman & Mary Winston   29655   2.95
If you always thought you had to sacrifice eating enjoyment for good health—think again!
Contains hundreds of flavor-tested recipes...with good health and good eating in mind.

____ **THE-SAVE-YOUR-LIFE-DIET, David Reuben, M.D.**   29678   2.50
A nationwide bestseller...will tell you how to protect yourself from six of the most serious
diseases of American life.

____ **THE SAVE-YOUR-LIFE-DIET HIGH-FIBER COOKBOOK**
David Reuben, M.D., & Barbara Reuben, M.S.   29820   2.75
The first authentic high fiber cookbook! Delicious health giving recipes from the Doctor
who revolutionized American's eating habits.

BB   **BALLANTINE MAIL SALES**
      Dept. TA, 201 E. 50th St., New York, N.Y. 10022

Please send me the BALLANTINE or DEL REY BOOKS I have
checked above. I am enclosing $ . . . . (add 50¢ per copy to
cover postage and handling). Send check or money order — no
cash or C.O.D.'s please. Prices and numbers are subject to change
without notice.

Name_____

Address_____

City_____State_____Zip Code_____

25   Allow at least 4 weeks for delivery.   TA-2